DIVINE COMEDY

RETHINKING THE PRESENT DAY.

MAWPHNIANG NAPOLEON

Copyright © Mawphniang Napoleon
All Rights Reserved.

This book has been self-published with all reasonable efforts taken to make the material error-free by the author. No part of this book shall be used, reproduced in any manner whatsoever without written permission from the author, except in the case of brief quotations embodied in critical articles and reviews.

The Author of this book is solely responsible and liable for its content including but not limited to the views, representations, descriptions, statements, information, opinions and references ["Content"]. The Content of this book shall not constitute or be construed or deemed to reflect the opinion or expression of the Publisher or Editor. Neither the Publisher nor Editor endorse or approve the Content of this book or guarantee the reliability, accuracy or completeness of the Content published herein and do not make any representations or warranties of any kind, express or implied, including but not limited to the implied warranties of merchantability, fitness for a particular purpose. The Publisher and Editor shall not be liable whatsoever for any errors, omissions, whether such errors or omissions result from negligence, accident, or any other cause or claims for loss or damages of any kind, including without limitation, indirect or consequential loss or damage arising out of use, inability to use, or about the reliability, accuracy or sufficiency of the information contained in this book.

Made with ♥ on the Notion Press Platform
www.notionpress.com

Dear reader,

this book is dedicated to you.

Your unwavering support and encouragement have made this journey possible.

Thank you for being a part of .

Contents

Contents

Foreword

"It is with great pride and honor that we present to you Divine Comedy 2.0 by Mawphniang Napoleon. This modern retelling of Dante's classic work is a testament to the timelessness of the themes explored in the original. Through the lens of the author's imagination, this edition adds new elements and stories to the timeless tale of hope, love, faith, free will, destiny, grief, and significance in the afterlife. With chapters including The Wandering Poet, The Journey of Dante, The Tapestry of Fate, Dante's Path, The Journey's Grace, and The Phantom's Journey, this book guides the reader through the different circles of hell and heaven in a contemporary setting. We hope that you will find this first edition to be a thought-provoking and inspiring journey, and we look forward to seeing the author's future additions to this timeless masterpiece."

A Team

Preface

"We are honored to present to you the modern version of Dante's timeless classic, "Divine Comedy 2.0" by Mawphniang Napoleon. This first edition takes the timeless tale of "The Divine Comedy" and adds new insights, stories, and perspectives for the contemporary reader. The book explores themes of faith, love, free will, destiny, grief, hope, and the afterlife through the journey of the wandering poet Dante. With its imaginative take on the different circles of hell and heaven in the modern world, "Divine Comedy 2.0" offers a fresh and captivating look at one of the greatest works of all time. We hope this book will inspire and entertain you, dear reader, and look forward to the author's continued contributions to this new version of Dante's epic tale."

Acknowledgements

"We are deeply grateful to all of our readers, family, friends, and even those who may consider us their foes. Your support, encouragement, and criticism have been instrumental in shaping this book. We also offer our thanks to Dante Alighieri for his timeless masterpiece, "The Divine Comedy," which has been a source of inspiration and reflection for us. The ups and downs of life have taught us invaluable lessons and helped us to grow, and we are honored to share our philosophical musings with you in this book. We hope it brings you insight, enjoyment, and contemplation."

Prologue

"It is with great honor that we present to you Divine Comedy 2.0 by Mawphniang Napoleon. This modern retelling of Dante's classic work takes the timeless journey of The Divine Comedy and infuses it with new interpretations, stories, and perspectives. In this first edition, readers will be transported through time, faith, love, hope, and the ever-present themes of free will and destiny. Join the wandering poet as he travels through the different circles of hell, up to the heights of heaven, and back again in search of meaning, significance, and grace. Get ready to be captivated by Dante's journey through the ages and immerse yourself in the tapestry of fate that is Divine Comedy 2.0."

Special Note

"Please note that this book is meant to be a work of fiction and comedy and is not intended to cause offense to anyone. The author sincerely apologizes to anyone who may be affected by the contents of this book. If anyone has any objections or concerns regarding names, places, or terms used in the book, they are kindly requested to contact the author at malung3@gmail.com. The purpose of this book is to educate and raise awareness and any offense caused is unintended."

One More Note

"Dear readers, come with a pen and paper in hand,

To mark the errors that may be at hand,

Laugh and chuckle as you read each page,

For this book will bring smiles on every age.

With each rhyme and verse, you'll surely smile,

As jokes and puns run rampant all the while,

Your sides will ache with laughter, that's for sure,

And you'll thank the heavens for this comedy tour.

So don't be shy, mark down each mistake,

And enjoy the laughter that it will make,

And if you find a joke that's really great,

Be sure to share it with a friend or mate.

So sit back, relax, and let the fun begin,

This funny sonnet's just about to win."

1. The Wandering Poet: A Journey Through Time, Faith, and Love

Dante woke up from his slumber in Ravenna's tomb

With confusion in his mind and love in his heart

He thought of Beatrice, Virgil, and Saint Bernard

But they were nowhere to be found, all lost in time

So he wandered to the streets of Vatican City

And saw the changes that the centuries had wrought

The Westminster faith, Nicaea Creed, all so strange

A world that was so different from his time

He questioned the changing of time and faith's position

The different versions of the Bible, translation so vast

The Vulgate, once so revered, now ancient and ignored

The development of Christianity, a faith that's changed

The killing in the name of God, the denominations so many

Each with their own dogmas, doctrines, so confusing

Religion dividing humanity, for the sake of power's few

The Grand Inquisitor, the hungry for control, rule all

Dante traveled through the busy market of Bombay

Young Bazarov, a world that was so new and strange

He saw the divide, the confusion, the chaos of modern days

A world so different from his time, so far away

Amidst the chaos and confusion, Dante journeyed on

His heart aching for the love that once was his

A world so different from his time, so far gone

A quest to find the truth, to find what is

He wondered at the changes that time had wrought

The killing in the name of God, the divisions of faith

Religion dividing humanity, for the sake of power's few

The Grand Inquisitor, the hungry for control, rule all

And yet, in the darkness of this world, there still was love

A light that shone through the confusion and strife

A beacon that called to him, a guiding hand from above

A hope that amidst the chaos, there still was life

He journeyed on, through the crowded market's throng

His heart heavy with the weight of what he saw

The corruption, the greed, the lust for power so strong

A world so different from the one he knew before .

Dante found himself all alone in the busy city of Dis

A world so different from his time, so lost in modernity

The people were busy, staring and scrolling at a mysterious glass

A modern act of sorcery, where text and images appeared in their hands

He saw them trying to be like gods, with their eyes fixed on the screen

Their minds consumed by the endless stream of information

They sought the elixir of knowledge, the secrets of the universe

But all they found was a shallow reflection of reality

Dante questioned the meaning of it all, what was the purpose

Of this endless pursuit of knowledge and power, this race to be like gods

What was the cost of this obsession, this thirst for the elixir

Did it bring them closer to the truth, or was it just a mirage

He saw the emptiness in their eyes, the lack of true connection

The emptiness of a life lived in the shadow of the glass

A life devoid of love and meaning, a life of mere consumption

A world so different from the one he knew, so dark and bleak

And yet, he wondered, was there still hope in this land of Cocytus

Could love and truth still be found, amidst the chaos and confusion

The journey of Dante, a pilgrimage of faith and love

A quest to find the heart of God, in the midst of humanity's strife.

But as he looked around, the doubts crept in his mind

A pessimism that threatened to consume him whole

He saw the people, lost in their screens, trapped in their own kind

And wondered if the truth was just a myth, a tale so old

He wondered if the elixir was just a pipe dream, a false notion

A tool used by the powerful to keep the masses in line

A false promise of knowledge, a mirage of truth and devotion

A trap that kept the people from ever truly shining

And so, Dante journeyed on, through the land of Cocytus

His heart heavy with the weight of what he saw

The emptiness, the loneliness, the lack of true connection

A world so different from the one he knew, so dark and bleak

Dante found himself all alone in the streets of Vatican City

A world so different from his time, so lost in modernity

He saw a dirty wall, painted with text that caught his eye

Words that he did not recognize, a surprise to his curiosity

The wall displayed the words of Jorge Luis Borges

"Dante and Shakespeare divide the world between them. There is no third."

A philosophical musing, a statement of fact or fiction

It made Dante ponder, what was the truth and what was lies

Was he truly a divider of the world, a creator of distinction

Or was he just a man, who wrote of his own redemption

The journey of Dante, a pilgrimage of faith and love

A quest to find the heart of God, in the midst of humanity's strife

Perhaps the epigraph to The Divine Comedy itself should be

"Gather inspiration all ye who enter here."

A call to all who seek truth, a beacon of hope in the night

A reminder that the journey is not just about the destination

But as Dante looked around, he saw a world in decline

A world lost in its own darkness, a world devoid of light

He wondered if his words still held any weight, any meaning
Or if they were just forgotten, a distant memory fading
He wondered if the truth he sought was just a pipe dream
A false notion, a tool used by the powerful to keep the masses in line
A false promise of knowledge, a mirage of truth and devotion
A trap that kept the people from ever truly shining.
Dante heard a strange loudspeaker blaring the words "Tynghung"
Words that blamed him for the intellectual revolutions to come
Words that claimed that his writing in the vernacular allowed ideas to take wide root
Words that spoke of his role in the Renaissance, Reformation, and Enlightenment
He listened in disbelief, as they accused him of undermining the Church
Of advocating that reading the Bible in one's own vernacular meant individual understanding
Of outright inventing elements of the cosmology presented in The Divine Comedy
Words that cast him as the villain, the one who set the stage for dissent
He stood there, in the street, listening to the loudspeaker's blame
Wondering if the truth he wrote was still relevant, still true
Wondering if the ideas he presented, were still worth the same
Wondering if his words were just forgotten, lost in the dust of time
He thought of his journey, a pilgrimage of faith and love
A quest to find the heart of God, in the midst of humanity's strife
He thought of the truth he sought, the truth he wrote of
And wondered if it still held any weight, any meaning in life
They said that Protestant leaders advocated
The reading of the Bible in one's own vernacular too as a way to understand
But what did that mean for Dante, the one who started it all
Did it mean his legacy was lost, his ideas cast aside, no longer grand
And so, Dante journeyed on, his heart heavy with the weight of blame

A world so different from his time, a world so lost in modernity
He wondered if his words still held any value, any truth still the same
In a world where ideas and truth are constantly redefined.

2. The Journey of Dante: A Timeless Tale of Hope and Love

Dante, the bard of Florentine days,
Did question his own heart and soul with dread,
His Divine Comedy, a work of art,
Had brought confusion to the masses' heart,
And he himself was plagued with self-doubt,
As to whether his ideas had brought about
A good or evil, a light or a dark,
Influence upon the people who embark
On the journey through the realms divine,
And did his vernacular cloud the mind,
Of those who sought truth and wisdom's way,
Or did it lead them to a false display?
His heart and soul, both heavy with regret,
Wondered if his works had truly met
The expectations of the people's call,
Or had they only brought a greater fall,
To those who sought the truth within his rhyme,
Did it lead them to a life of crime?
And as the masses questioned his intent,
Did they forget that he was but a lent
Prophet, a messenger of the divine,
Whose words were meant to be a line
Of guidance, and not a weapon of hate,
Or did they use his words to seal their fate?
His thoughts, once pure and filled with grace,
Had become the subject of the people's debate,

And as he looked upon the world with sorrow,
Did he regret the power of his vernacular,
That had brought confusion to the masses' mind,
And made his work seem more of a bind?
The bard of Florentine days, Dante,
Did question his own heart and soul with dread,
Wondering if his words had truly been
A guidance to the people's quest for the divine,
Or had they been the cause of greater harm,
And caused the people to question his charm?
if there was still hope for humanity, if love could conquer all
He wondered if there was still a chance for the world to heal
And as he walked on, he felt a glimmer of hope in his heart
A belief that amidst the chaos, love would triumph over all
Dante's journey through time and space, a pilgrimage of faith
A quest to find the truth, to find what is really real
A search for meaning, for love, for a world that's lost its way
A journey to find the heart of God, amidst humanity's strife
And as he continued on, he knew that he would never give up
For as long as there was hope, as long as there was love
He would journey on, he would continue his search
For the truth, for the heart of God, amidst humanity's strife.
The journey of Dante, a timeless tale of hope and love
A tale that speaks to the ages, a tale that will never grow old
A tale of courage, of faith, of a man's quest for truth
A tale that will inspire generations, a tale that will never be told.
And so, Dante continued on his journey, through the land of Cocytus
With a heart full of love and a mind full of wonder
He sought to find the truth in this world of chaos and confusion
And to bring light to the darkness, to offer hope to the lost.
He encountered many challenges along the way, many obstacles to overcome

But he persevered, his faith never wavering, his heart always beating strong
For he knew that the journey was not just about the destination
But about the growth and transformation that he would undergo.

• 8 •

3. The Tapestry of Fate: Dante's Journey Through Free Will and Destiny

In the depths of his soul, Dante ponders fate,

The weight of his actions, and the choices he made.

He grapples with the concepts of freewill and predestination,

Wondering if his destiny was set from the start,

Or if his life was shaped by the choices of his heart.

His past life flashes before him, a tapestry woven tight,

With threads of choice and circumstance, a daunting sight.

He recalls the roads he took, and those he left behind,

And wonders if his steps were guided, or his own design.

The thought of predestination chills him to the bone,

As he ponders the possibility that he's not alone,

That his fate was predetermined, his choices just an act,

Leaving him powerless, his future set in stone, in fact.

Yet, Dante clings to the notion of freewill with all his might,

Believing that he's in control, with the power to choose right.

He refuses to accept that his fate was sealed in the past,

And instead, chooses to forge his own path, to make it last.

He searches for answers, in the depths of his mind,

And contemplates the meaning of life, and what he'll find.

Is it his fate to wander, lost in this dark wood,

Or is it his choice, that determined his life's course, as it should.

In the end, Dante realizes, that his fate and his choices intertwine,

That his destiny is shaped by the roads he takes, and the signs.

And so, he moves forward, with the power to choose,

Embracing his freewill, and his life's purpose to pursue.

And in his journey, Dante finds solace in the thought,

That his fate is not set, and his choices can be brought

To bear on his life, to shape his destiny, to be.

The past may have its hold, but the present and future are free,

And Dante embraces this, embracing his humanity.

For he knows that he's the master of his own fate,

And his choices, his actions, will determine his final state.

No longer burdened by the weight of predestination,

Dante walks with confidence, towards his destination.

And though his path may be long, and the way may be rough,

He knows that his choices, his freewill, will make it enough.

For he has learned, that fate and freewill are not separate,

But intertwined, like the threads of a delicate weave of fate.

And in the end, he knows, that his life was always his to make,

That his choices and actions, determined his destiny's fate.

So Dante moves forward, with the knowledge of his worth,

Embracing his freewill, and his own unique birth.

For he knows that he's the master of his own fate,

And his choices, his actions, will determine his final state.

And as he walks, he leaves behind the worries of his past,

For he knows that his future, is his own to grasp.

And though the road ahead may be uncertain and steep,

Dante moves forward, with a heart that's light and free.

For he knows that fate may guide him, but his choices will steer,

And his actions will shape the life, he holds so dear.

And so, he walks with purpose, towards his destiny's call,

Embracing his freewill, and standing tall.

And though his path may cross with twists and turns ahead,

Dante knows, that his choices will see him through, till the end.

For he has learned that his fate is not set, but in his hands,

And his choices, his actions, will shape his final strands.

So Dante moves forward, with a heart full of hope,

Embracing his freewill, and his life's endless scope.

For he knows that his fate is his own to make,

And his choices, his actions, will determine his final state.

And as he walks, he carries with him the wisdom of the past,

And the knowledge that his future, is not set in stone, at last.

And though his journey may be difficult, and his steps may falter,

Dante knows that his freewill, will be his ultimate alter.

For he has learned that his fate and his choices coexist,

And that his actions will shape his future, as he persists.

And so, he walks with grace, towards his destiny's dawn,

Embracing his freewill, and moving on.

And though the road ahead may be shrouded in mystery,

Dante knows that his choices will bring clarity.

For he has learned that his fate is not predetermined,

But shaped by the actions of his heart, his choices, his hand, unbinned.

So Dante moves forward, with a heart full of love,

Embracing his freewill, and his life's gift from above.

For he knows that his fate is his own to make,

And his choices, his actions, will determine his final state.

4. Dante's Path: A Journey Through Grief and Hope

Dante walks through the streets of Ri Bhoi,

remembering his wife Gemma Donati

and his beloved children, lost in time

as he journeys towards Florence's prime.

His heart aches for their embrace,

yet he knows they've moved on without trace.

His mind drifts to his father Alieghiero,

whose love and guidance he'll always hold dear-o.

Alieghiero Di Bellincione, a man of grace,

who taught him the ways of life's true race.

But now, he too, is gone from this place,

leaving Dante with a void to erase.

The thought of never seeing them again

brings Dante to a state of pain.

He wishes for a miracle, a sign,

that his loved ones are just waiting to find

him, to reunite as a family divine.

But reality hits him, and he's left to pine.

Philosophy creeps into his mind,

as he wonders if this is how life's designed.

Is it just a cycle of birth and death,

with love and loss taking the final breadth?

Or is there a purpose to all this strife,

a reason for this eternal battle of life?

Dante cannot help but feel pessimistic,

as he realizes he may never exist with them.

His journey may lead him to a different end,
leaving his heart in an eternal bend.
But despite the doubts and fears that he faces,
he continues on, searching for divine graces.
So he walks on, through the streets of Ri Bhoi,
hoping that someday, his love will come to him.
Remembering Gemma, his children, and Alieghiero,
as he makes his way to Florence's glowing hero.
And though the future may seem uncertain,
he'll keep searching, for love is eternal, aye verily.
Dante's thoughts are a whirlwind of emotion,
as he reflects on life's great devotion.
He recalls his wife's smile, his children's laughter,
and his father's wise words that came thereafter.
But now, they are gone, and he is alone,
forced to face life's battles on his own.
He wonders if he'll ever see them again,
if their memories will continue to sustain.
Will he ever find the answers he seeks,
or will he forever remain incomplete?
The questions weigh heavily on his mind,
leaving him feeling lost and confined.
But he knows that he must push on,
for his loved ones, who are forever gone.
For they wouldn't want him to give up hope,
to surrender to life's constant scope.
So he walks on, with a heavy heart,
searching for a way to make a fresh start.
And as he walks, he sees a flicker of light,
casting a shadow on his weary sight.
It brings him comfort, and he knows he's on track,

for his loved ones, who are watching his back.

And though they may never be by his side,

their love will forever be his guide.

So he walks on, towards Florence's shining gates,

searching for the love that forever awaits.

With every step, he feels closer to home,

and he knows that he'll never feel alone.

For his loved ones are always with him,

as he makes his way to the end of life's dim.

And so, Dante continues on his journey,

with a heart full of love and a mind full of queries.

He knows that life will not always be easy,

but he has faith that he'll find what he seeks.

For though his loved ones are gone from sight,

he knows that their love will guide him to the light.

5. The Journey's Grace

As he trudged along the scorching path,

He gazed upon the endless fields of dust,

A world of emptiness that seems to last,

With not a soul to ease his weary mind,

And every step he took, just seemed so wrong.

He felt as though his spirit was cast,

Into a land of bitter pain and pain,

Where every thought, was just another test,

To prove his worth, or prove his worthlessness.

And still the sun, it beat upon his skin,

With scorching heat, that seared and burned within,

His soul, his flesh, his very being felt,

The torments of this world, that seemed so real.

And just as he began to lose his faith,

He met a man, his guide Virgil

in robes of gleaming white,

A man, who looked as though he had the grace,

To understand the pain, that he concealed.

This man, he spoke in words of comfort, calm,

And whispered tales, of ancient wisdom, calm,

That held within, the answers to his quest,

And gave him hope, in this land of the blessed.

And so he followed, through the fields of dust,

With trust, and faith, that this man held the truth,

And as they walked, they talked, of life, of death,

Of all the mysteries, that lay beyond,

The limits of the earth, and sky above,

And as they walked, he felt his spirit lift,
And slowly, he began to understand,
The reasons for his journey, and his quest.
And as the sun began to set, at last,
He saw the city, shining in the light,
The city of his dreams, that seemed so far,
A city filled with peace, and hope, and love,
And as he entered, he felt his soul transform,
And all his doubts, and fears, they seemed to fade,
And he knew, that he had found his way,
And all his wandering, was not in vain.
And as he walked the streets of shining gold,
He saw the wonders of this holy place,
A place of beauty, and of grace untold,
Where all his troubles, seemed to fade away.

6. The Phantom's Journey: Dante's Search for Significance in the Afterlife

As he traversed through the realms of the afterlife,

Dante pondered the questions of life and death.

He yearned to know the truth of his existence,

And sought guidance from the shade of Virgil.

Virgil, a wise and learned spirit,

Taught Dante of the complexities of life.

He explained that the living can never truly see,

The ghosts that roam the realms of the afterlife.

Dante was taken aback by this revelation,

For he had believed that his journey was not in vain.

He asked Virgil, "Is there no way to make myself known,

To the living, to make them see that I still exist?"

Virgil replied, "Alas, Dante, it is not so simple,

For the living are bound by time, while the dead are free.

Your spirit remains, but it is not enough,

For the living see only what they want to see."

Dante sighed and pondered the weight of this truth,

His heart heavy with the realization of his fate.

He asked, "Then what is the meaning of life,

What is the purpose of this journey that I undertake?"

Virgil replied, "The meaning of life, Dante, is subjective,

It is a quest for each soul to find its own truth.

It is about the experiences we have, the lessons we learn,

And the legacy we leave for those who come after us."

And so, Dante continued on his journey,

Embracing his ghostly form and seeking the truth.

He learned and grew, and found his own meaning,

Leaving behind a legacy of wisdom and understanding.

Though he may have been forgotten by the living,

His spirit remains, a constant reminder of the past.

And though his journey may have been long and hard,

It was not in vain, for he had found his purpose at last.

So let us remember Dante, the wandering ghost,

And the lessons he learned on his journey through life.

For his spirit remains, a beacon of hope,

Teaching us all the meaning of existence and the truth.

For he had believed that his voyage was not in futility.

He inquired of Virgil, "Why do they not perceive me?

Am I so trivial that I am but a phantom?"

Virgil replied with a sagacious tenor, "Dante, you comprehend,

The world has progressed and you are left behind.

Your physical form may have perished, but your essence persists.

But to the living, you are but a nostalgic apparition,

A transient recollection, a shade of what once was.

You must grasp, Dante, that this is the nature of existence.

It is a harsh truth, but it is the veracity you must confront."

Dante gazed upon Virgil with despondency in his optics,

His heart weighed down by the gravity of his newfound comprehension.

He queried, "Is there no means to make myself palpable to the living?

Can I not inspire them to see that I am still here, that I still endure?"

Virgil responded, "I am sorry to say, Dante, that this is not possible.

For the living, time progresses, and the deceased are but memories.

But do not be disheartened, for your journey is not in futility.

You are here to learn, to behold, to comprehend the significance of life.

And though the living may not see you, your essence persists,

A beacon of hope and direction for those who will succeed you."
Dante nodded, accepting his newfound truth,
But still feeling the burden of his past and his loss.
He looked to Virgil and asked, "What is the significance of life?
What is the purpose of my journey and the rest of the deceased?"
Virgil replied, "That is a question that has plagued sages for ages.
It is a question that may never truly be answered, Dante, for the significance of life is subjective,
And varies from individual to individual, from spirit to spirit.
But you must discover your own significance, Dante, and make it your own.
For the journey of life is not solely about what we behold,
But about the encounters we have, the lessons we learn, and the inheritance we leave.
And so, Dante, you must persist on your journey,
To learn, to grow, and to find your own veracity.
For even though you may be a phantom, your essence persists,
A constant reminder of the lessons of the past.
And though the living may never see you, your journey is not in futility,
For your journey is about more than just what others can behold."
So Dante persisted, with a newfound comprehension and purpose,
Embracing his ghostly form, and learning the significance of life.
And though he may have been forgotten by the living, his essence persists,
A constant reminder of the lessons of the past.
And though his journey may have been lengthy and arduous, it was not in futility,
For he had discovered his own significance, and left his inheritance behind.
Virgil led Dante to the valley of U Lumsohpetbneng,
A place where the tormented souls do dwell.
Here, they sought the gate of Hell,
A place of endless suffering and pain.
But before they entered, they stopped to drink,

Quenching their thirst at the banks of Umiam lake.

Dante and Virgil were on a quest to find Beatrice and those who had passed before them.

As they journeyed, their path was redirected by the ferryman, Acheron.

With a flick of his hand, he presented to them the tome of Hunefer,

The book of death, a guide to the underworld, where Judas resides as its gatekeeper.

Judas, the traitor, was the caretaker of this place,

Guarding the gate with a steadfast hand.

His eyes were dark, his demeanor cold,

As he watched the souls of the damned.

Virgil approached him, seeking passage through,

For they were on a mission, a journey to undertake.

Judas spoke not a word, but gestured with a nod,

Allowing them to enter the realm of the lost.

And as they descended into the depths of Hell,

Virgil spoke to Dante of the meaning of life.

"The journey we undertake is not just about what we see,

But about the experiences we have, the lessons we learn."

And though the journey was treacherous and grim,

The lessons that Dante learned were invaluable.

For it was in this place, where he found redemption,

And understood the purpose of his quest.

And though his soul may have been stained with sin,

His spirit remains, a constant reminder of the past.

For life is not just about what we see,

But about the choices we make and the paths we choose.

And though we may wander in the shadows of our past,

Our spirit remains, a beacon of hope and truth.

For even in the depths of Hell, there is a glimmer of light,

A reminder of the lessons we must learn and the journey we must undertake.

So let us heed the words of Virgil,

The wise and learned spirit who guided Dante's way.

For his teachings still hold relevance today,

As we seek to find the meaning of life and its goal.

For life is a journey, not a destination,

A quest for knowledge and personal growth.

And though we may never truly know,

The answer to the eternal question of life.

Dante was filled with fear and trepidation, as he held the book in his hands.

For the journey ahead was dark, shrouded in mystery and unknown horrors.

But Virgil was steadfast, his resolve unshaken by the ominous task ahead.

He reassured Dante that they must continue, to seek out the truth and find their loved ones.

The air was thick with the scent of brimstone and the sounds of unearthly moans.

They made their way through the treacherous landscape, guided by the book of Hunefer.

Through the darkness, they encountered strange creatures, lost souls and spirits in pain.

And as they journeyed deeper into the underworld, Dante felt the weight of their purpose.

7. The First Circle: Social Media Addiction

In the first circle of the modern Hell , known as 'ka Niamra ba nyngkong'
Lies a realm of souls in constant spell
Addicted to the screens that consume their days
And the validation that they crave in ways

They scroll and scroll, a never-ending quest
For likes, shares, and comments, they do their best
To present a perfect image, a facade
Of a life that's not quite as it seems abroad

They're the Narcissus of our modern age
Trapped in their own reflection, on a page
Of social media, where they're never alone
But always seeking validation to hone

Their images, their thoughts, their very souls
In this first circle, they take their tolls
On the mind and heart, in a constant state
Of self-obsession, it's their own fate

To wander here, in this digital abyss
With no escape from the likes and the diss
They're the ones who've lost their way in time
In this first circle, they pay their dime

For the sins of vanity and self-indulgence

They're the victims of their own indulgence
In the endless cycle of the digital world
Where they're forever trapped, in a swirl

Of notifications and constant updates
Their souls are lost, in this digital fate

The names of these souls, they're known to us all
Like Cleopatra, who fell for her own call
Of vanity, and the need for attention
She's trapped here, in this digital detention

Or Julius Caesar, whose ego was grand
He too, fell for the social media command
And now, he wanders here, in this first circle
Trapped in a cycle, that's forever purgle

Or the great Shakespeare, whose words were divine
But in this digital world, he's lost his shine
And now, he's trapped, in this endless scroll
Where his words, they're no longer whole

In the first circle, of the 21st-century Hell
Lies a realm of souls, in a constant spell
Of social media addiction, and the need
For validation, that they'll forever feed.

And as they wander in this digital abyss
They're met with the screams and the sighs and the hiss
Of the souls who've come before, and have found
That this is a cycle, that can't be unbound

They're the ones who've lost their way in time
In this first circle, they pay their dime
For the sins of vanity and self-indulgence
They're the victims of their own indulgence

They're met with the cries of Marie Antoinette
Who was brought down by her vanity, and the net
Of social media, that she couldn't escape
And now, she's trapped, in this endless shape

Or the great Napoleon, whose ego was grand
He too, fell for the social media command
And now, he wanders here, in this first circle
Trapped in a cycle, that's forever purgle

And as they wander, they're met with the sight
Of the great Dante himself, who had insight
Into the dangers of the digital age
And now, he's trapped, in this endless rage

He wrote of Hell, and its many circles
But never did he dream, of this digital purgle
Where souls are lost, in a constant scroll
And the cycle, it never ends, it's a toll

This is the first circle, of the 21st-century Hell
Where souls are punished, for their addiction to dwell
In the digital world, where they're never alone
But always seeking validation, to hone

Their images, their thoughts, their very souls
In this first circle, they take their tolls
On the mind and heart, in a constant state
Of self-obsession, it's their own fate

So beware, dear souls, of the digital age
And the dangers that it can rage
For in this first circle, you'll be trapped
In a cycle, that can never be un-wrapped.

And as they wander, they're met with the sight
Of the great Mark Twain, who had insight
Into the dangers of the digital age
And now, he's trapped, in this endless rage

He wrote of the human condition, and the soul
But never did he dream, of this digital hole
Where souls are lost, in a constant scroll
And the cycle, it never ends, it's a toll

This is the first circle, of the 21st-century Hell
Where souls are punished, for their addiction to dwell
In the digital world, where they're never alone
But always seeking validation, to hone

Their images, their thoughts, their very souls
In this first circle, they take their tolls
On the mind and heart, in a constant state
Of self-obsession, it's their own fate

So beware, dear souls, of the digital age

And the dangers that it can rage
For in this first circle, you'll be trapped
In a cycle, that can never be un-wrapped.

They're met with the cries of Oscar Wilde
Who was brought down by his vanity, and the piles
Of social media, that he couldn't escape
And now, he's trapped, in this endless shape

Or the great Virginia Woolf, whose words were divine
But in this digital world, she's lost her shine
And now, she's trapped, in this endless scroll
Where her words, they're no longer whole

In this first circle, of the 21st-century Hell
Lies a realm of souls, in a constant spell
Of social media addiction, and the need
For validation, that they'll forever feed.

They're met with the screams of William Golding
Who wrote of the human condition, and the holding
Of the soul, but never did he dream, of this digital hole
Where souls are lost, in a constant scroll

This is the first circle, of the 21st-century Hell
Where souls are punished, for their addiction to dwell
In the digital world, where they're never alone
But always seeking validation, to hone

Their images, their thoughts, their very souls
In this first circle, they take their tolls

On the mind and heart, in a constant state
Of self-obsession, it's their own fate.

As they wander, they're met with the sight
Of the great George Orwell, who had insight
Into the dangers of the digital age
And now, he's trapped, in this endless rage

He wrote of the dangers of surveillance and control
But never did he dream, of this digital hold
Where souls are lost, in a constant scroll
And the cycle, it never ends, it's a toll

This is the first circle, of the 21st-century Hell
Where souls are punished, for their addiction to dwell
In the digital world, where they're never alone
But always seeking validation, to hone

Their images, their thoughts, their very souls
In this first circle, they take their tolls
On the mind and heart, in a constant state
Of self-obsession, it's their own fate

So beware, dear souls, of the digital age
And the dangers that it can rage
For in this first circle, you'll be trapped
In a cycle, that can never be un-wrapped

They're met with the cries of Fyodor Dostoevsky
Who wrote of the human condition, and the key
To the soul, but never did he dream, of this digital hole

Where souls are lost, in a constant scroll

This is the first circle, of the 21ˢᵗ-century Hell
Where souls are punished, for their addiction to dwell
In the digital world, where they're never alone
But always seeking validation, to hone

Their images, their thoughts, their very souls
In this first circle, they take their tolls
On the mind and heart, in a constant state
Of self-obsession, it's their own fate

As they wander, they're met with the sight
Of the great Edgar Allan Poe, who had insight
Into the darkness of the human mind
But never did he dream, of this digital bind

Where souls are lost, in a constant scroll
And the cycle, it never ends, it's a toll
In this first circle, of the 21ˢᵗ-century Hell
Where souls are punished, for their addiction to dwell
In the digital world, where they're never alone
But always seeking validation, to hone
Their images, their thoughts, their very souls
In this first circle, they take their tolls
On the mind and heart, in a constant state
Of self-obsession, it's their own fate.

As they wander, they're met with the sight
Of the great J.R.R. Tolkien, who had insight
Into the power of imagination and fantasy

But never did he dream, of this digital insanity

Where souls are lost, in a constant scroll
And the cycle, it never ends, it's a toll
In this first circle, of the 21ˢᵗ-century Hell
Where souls are punished, for their addiction to dwell
In the digital world, where they're never alone
But always seeking validation, to hone
Their images, their thoughts, their very souls
In this first circle, they take their tolls
On the mind and heart, in a constant state
Of self-obsession, it's their own fate.

They're met with the cries of Leo Tolstoy
Who wrote of the human condition, and the joy
Of the soul, but never did he dream, of this digital hole
Where souls are lost, in a constant scroll

In the digital realm, a first circle of Hell
Souls are trapped, in a constant spell
Of addiction, to screens and validation
In a never-ending quest, of self-obsession

Famous figures, like Cleopatra and Caesar
Fall victim to the cycle, a digital purgatory
Their vanity and self-indulgence, their sin
Trapped in this cycle, forever to spin

Shakespeare and Dante, both with insight
Are now trapped, in this digital plight
Marie Antoinette, Napoleon, and Wilde

All fell for the social media command, and are piled

In this abyss, with no way out
Their souls, forever in doubt
Beware dear souls, of the digital age
For in this first circle, you'll be trapped in a cage

Of self-obsession and validation addiction
A cycle that can never be un-wrapped, with conviction.

8. The Second Circle: Environmental Destruction

As they wander through the abyss of Hell
They reach the second circle, where the tales foretell , known as 'ka Niamra ba
ar'
Of souls who've wrought destruction and harm
To the earth, in their own self-centered charm

They're met with the cries of Genghis Khan
Who ravaged the land, and caused a ban
On the planet's resources, now he endures
In this second circle, his own curses

Or the grand Cleopatra, whose vanity
Led to the devastation of the Nile's fertility
And now, she wanders here, in this second sphere
Trapped in a cycle, that's forever queer

As they wander, they see the great Alexander
Who held might, but not the foresight to protect the earth
Now he's trapped in this endless dearth
For the environmental fires he failed to quell

And the Industrial Revolutionists too
Who thought only of progress, and the lists
Of profits to be made, now they see
The destruction they've caused in this second degree

In this second circle of the 21st-century Hell
Lies a realm of souls, in a constant spell
Of environmental destruction, and the need
For action that they'll forever heed

They're met with the cries of John D. Rockefeller
Who exploited natural resources, and caused a shocker
To the planet, and now, he's trapped
In this cycle that's forever wrapped

And the great Henry Ford, who had insight
Into the power of industry and progress
But never did he dream of the environmental mess
That his actions would leave, in this endless plight

The cries of Donald Trump echo in the air
Who denied climate change, and caused a bump
To the planet, and now, he's trapped
In this cycle that's forever wrapped

And the great Joseph Stalin, who held might
But not the foresight to preserve the earth
And now, he's trapped, in this endless dearth
For the environmental blur he failed to quell

And Christopher Columbus too, who brought
Disease and destruction, to the human
And natural resources, and now, he's trapped
In this cycle that's forever wrapped

And the great Adolf Hitler, who held might

But not the foresight to preserve the earth
And now, he's trapped, in this endless dearth
For the environmental blur he failed to quell

In this second circle of the 21st-century Hell
Where souls are trapped, in a living hell
Forever wandering, in this realm of despair
For the sins of environmental care.

9. The Third Circle: Income Inequality

In the depths of the infernal abyss,

Where the souls of the damned forever dwell,

Lies the Third Circle, a place of Income Inequality, known as 'ka Niamra ba lai'

A reflection of the sins committed by the rich and mighty,

Who hoarded wealth and ignored the poor.

Ananias and Sapphira, Achan and Nabal,

Dives and Simon the Magician, King Ahab,

All suffer in this circle for their greed and envy,

Forced to endure eternal punishment for their neglect.

As Dante descends into this circle of Hell,

He is met by the spirit of Ananias,

A wealthy man from biblical times, who fell

Into the sin of greed and treachery.

Ananias and Sapphira, with their land sold,

Lied about the proceeds, choosing to hoard,

Their wealth and keep it from the poor,

And thus suffered the eternal consequences.

As Dante journeys deeper into this circle,

He meets the spirit of Achan,

A man from biblical times, who fell

Into the sin of greed and deception.

Achan, in his avarice, took forbidden spoils,
Bringing destruction upon his people and himself,
His punishment serves as a reminder of the ills
That come from greed and neglect of wealth.

Dante also encounters the spirit of Dives,
A wealthy man from the parable of Jesus,
Who ignored the cries of the poor man Lazarus,
And now suffers in eternal misery.

Nabal, in his arrogance, refused to share,
His wealth with David and his men,
And suffered the consequences of his greed,
As his punishment in this circle of Hell.

As Dante observes the punishment of these souls,
He reflects on the importance of charity and compassion,
For those who are less fortunate,
To avoid falling into the same fate as these souls of transgression.

Simon the Magician, a man who sought power,
And wealth, but ultimately fell into the sin of pride,
And now suffers in this circle of Hell for his deceit.

King Ahab, a man known for his greed and idolatry,
Suffers in eternal torment for his sins,
A reminder of the dangers of allowing wealth and power to control one's
destiny.

As Dante's journey in the Third Circle comes to an end,
He emerges with a newfound understanding,

Of the importance of compassion and charity,

And the need to aid the less fortunate, to avoid the eternal punishment of Income Inequality.

Dante looks back on the Third Circle,

Struck by the weight of the sins committed there,

And the eternal consequences that they bear.

But Dante's journey does not end here,

For there are still more circles of Hell to be explored,

And more lessons to be learned,

On the path to redemption and enlightenment.

May the Divine Comedy serve as a guide,

For all those who seek to understand the human condition,

And the consequences of our actions,

In this world and the next.

10. The Fourth Circle: Cyberbullying

In the depths of the infernal abyss,
Where the souls of the damned forever dwell,
Lies the Fourth Circle, a place of woe and stress, known as 'ka Niamra ba saw'
Where the sins of cyberbullying and online harm dwell.

Here, the souls of the cruel and callous,
Those who spread hate and caused harm online,
Are punished for their deeds and malice,
And forced to suffer forevermore.

The name of this circle is Cyberbullying,
A reflection of the sins committed here,
Where the souls torment and bully others,
And suffer the eternal consequences dear.

As Dante descends into this circle of hell,
He is met by the spirit of "Trollus",
A cyberbully from the modern age, who fell
Into the sin of spreading hate and causing harm online.

Trollus, along with many other like him,
Used the anonymity of the internet to spread their venom,
Choosing to torment and bully others,
And thus suffered the eternal consequences.

As Dante journeys deeper into this circle,

He meets the spirit of "Haxxor",
A hacker from the modern age, who fell
Into the sin of cybercrime and deception.

Haxxor, in his quest for power and control,
Invaded the privacy and security of others,
His punishment serves as a reminder of the ills
That come from cyberbullying and online harm.

In this circle of Hell, the souls of the cruel,
Are forever tortured for their sins,
Their punishment serves as a warning,
To those who would spread hate and cause harm online within.

As Dante observes the punishment of these souls,
He reflects on the importance of truth and integrity,
In the digital age, where misinformation can be spread so easily,
To avoid falling into the same fate as these souls of transgression.

As he continues his journey, Dante is determined,
To use the lessons he has learned,
To become a better person,
And to make a positive impact in the digital world.

May the Divine Comedy serve as a guide,
For all those who seek to understand the human condition,
And the consequences of our actions,
In this world and the next, including the online world.

And so, Dante's journey through the Fourth Circle,
Of Cyberbullying, comes to a close,

Leaving behind a lasting impression,
Of the dangers of cyberbullying and online harm,
And the importance of responsibility and empathy,
In the digital age, where technology and humanity intersect.

11. The Fifth Circle: Political Corruption

In the dark abyss, where the river of sorrow flows,
Lies the Fifth Circle, where the corrupt and vile souls,
Are submerged in a sea of boiling, putrid debris,
Punished for their sins of greed and treachery.

Here, the sinners writhe and scream in eternal pain,
Their cries echo through the eternal rain.
They are tormented by demons, who prod and poke,
For their role in political corruption, their hearts to provoke.

At the helm of this circle stands Machiavelli,
The master of manipulation, who delights in folly.
He guides the souls of the corrupt politicians,
Who used their power for personal ambitions.

With them swims the likes of Nixon and Stalin,
Whose deeds were stained with blood, like a salin.
They are tormented by demons, who prod and poke,
For their role in political corruption, and their hearts to provoke.

But not all are doomed to this fate,
For some seek redemption, before it's too late.
They repent for their sins and beg for forgiveness,
And with Dante's guidance, they may find release.

But the majority, however, remain in this plight,

Trapped in the Fifth Circle, day and night.
They are a cautionary tale, for all to see,
The consequences of political corruption, for eternity.

As Dante journeyed through this realm of woe,
We came upon a sight that made my heart to slow.
A group of souls, writhing in eternal pain,
Their screams echoing through the endless rain.

These were the corrupt leaders, who once held power,
But now, in death, they cower.
Their names are etched in infamy,
For their sins, they'll suffer eternally.

There was Julius Caesar, who sought to rule with might,
His ambition leading to the fall of Rome's light.
And Napoleon, who's greed knew no bounds,
His downfall, an echo of history's sounds.

We also saw the likes of Stalin and Hitler,
Their atrocities, a stain on humanity's glitter.
They too, are punished for their deeds of old,
Their souls, forever trapped in this cycle of cold.

But amidst the chaos, there was one who stood,
His eyes filled with a wisdom, that was both good and shrewd.
This was Socrates, the philosopher king,
His wisdom and virtue, a beacon in this dark thing.

He spoke to Dante with a voice that was clear,
"The corruption of power is a seed that will always seer.

But if we strive for virtue, and wisdom in our hearts,
We may avoid this fate, and a new path may start."

His words, a reminder that even in the darkest of places,
There is still hope, and a chance for grace.
But we must be vigilant, and strive to be true,
For the Fifth Circle of Hell, is not a fate we wish to pursue.

12. The Sixth Circle: Discrimination

In the Sixth Circle, where Discrimination reigns, known as 'ka Niamra ba hynriew'
Lies a realm of eternal pain, where souls are punished for their disdain
Towards those marginalized, cast in chains, Dante guides us through this circle of shame.

The Fascist Mussolini, forever to blame, bears eternal flame
For his discrimination, his soul in shame, as we journey through this Circle of Discrimination.

And the Czar Ivan, his heart made cruel, his fate is duel
For the oppression of the Russian serfs, a ghastly tool, in this realm of eternal pain.

The Queen Isabella, her legacy stained, for her persecution of indigenous peoples, her reign disdained
In the Sixth Circle, her soul is restrained, for her discrimination, forever pained.

As we delve deeper, we see souls in turmoil and swirl,
Condemned for their discrimination, a curse to unfurl, upon the marginalized, their actions a whirl.

The Pharaoh Ramses, his empire vast, endures eternal punishment, his legacy surpassed
For his treatment of the Israelites, a repast, in this realm of eternal pain.

The Nazi Hitler, a monster in human form, his soul is torn
For his persecution of the Jews, a hate born, in the depths of Hell, his soul is worn.

As we journey through this realm, we see souls in eternal despair
Condemned for their discrimination, a fate to ensnare, upon the marginalized, their actions a snare.

The Emperor Nero, his reign of terror, endures eternal punishment, his actions an error
For his persecution of the Christians, a horror, in this realm of eternal pain.

The Stalin, the dictator with iron will, his soul is still
For his persecution of the kulaks, his actions a thrill, in the depths of Hell, his soul is chill.

The Emperor Caligula, his reign of madness, endures eternal punishment, his actions a sadness
For his persecution of the senators, a gladness, in this realm of eternal pain.

The Pol Pot, the dictator with genocidal plans, his soul is in bans
For his persecution of the intellectuals, his actions a man's, in the depths of Hell, his soul is in stands.

We see Emperor Augustus, his reign of power, endures eternal punishment, his actions a sour
For his persecution of the Druids, a flower, in this realm of eternal pain.

The Mao Zedong, the dictator with cultural revolution, his soul is in confusion
For his persecution of the intellectuals and bourgeoisie, his actions a fusion, in

the depths of Hell, his soul is in profusion.

The Emperor Commodus, his reign of tyranny, endures eternal punishment, his actions a blasphemy
For his persecution of the gladiators, a tragedy, in this realm of eternal pain.

The Emperor Maxentius, his reign of oppression, endures eternal punishment, his actions a transgression
For his persecution of the Christians, a digression, in this realm of eternal pain.

The Kim Jong-un, the dictator with nuclear ambition, his soul is in submission
For his persecution of the dissidents, his actions a permission, in the depths of Hell, his soul is in conviction.

The Emperor Constantine, his reign of injustice, endures eternal punishment, his actions a misjudice
For his persecution of the pagans, a sacrifice, in this realm of eternal pain.

Suharto and Pinochet,
Their names forever etched in infamy, like a blot.
For their persecution of ethnic minorities and political opponents,
Their souls are now subject to ridicule and torment.

As they writhe in pain, surrounded by fire,
Their cries echo through the eternal mire.
They are tormented by demons, who prod and poke,
For their role in discrimination and oppression, and their hearts to provoke.

13. The Seventh Circle: Climate Change Denial

In the Seventh Circle of Hell, where sorrows and pain dwell, 'ka Niamra ba hynniew'
Lies the fate of souls who denied the climate change spell.
Their sins of omission, a grave moral transgression,
Condemned them to eternal suffering and oppression.

The first ring of this circle, a desert of burning sand,
Is reserved for those who spread misinformation and grandstanded.
Their false claims and deceit, now punished in this heat,
As they writhe in agony, unable to find a reprieve or retreat.

The second ring is a swamp of murky, diseased water,
Where those who profited off the earth's destruction now suffer.
They hoarded wealth and power, ignoring the impending hour,
Now they are trapped in this mire, forever to cower.

The third ring is a wasteland of crumbling ruins,
Where leaders who ignored the science, now pay their dues in.
Their apathy and inaction, now leads to devastation,
As they wander among the debris, in eternal lamentation.

In this circle of denial, Dante and Virgil now tread,
Guided by the spirit of Greta Thunberg, who spoke truth un-shed.
They pass by the tormented souls of Nero and Trump,
Whose legacy of denial, will forever be a dark stump.

But as they journey through this realm of eternal woe,
A glimmer of hope begins to softly glow.
For those who repent and take action, there is redemption,
A chance to break free from this cycle of damnation.

So let us learn from the mistakes of the past,
And take action to make sure this fate does not last.
For the sake of future generations, let us all strive,
To break free from the Seventh Circle, and truly come alive.

And so Dante and Virgil continue on their journey through the Seventh Circle,
Guided by the spirit of Thunberg, their guide and oracle.
They come across the soul of Plato, who in life was a sage,
But in death, he is punished for not acting on knowledge he had.

Next, they encounter the soul of Churchill, a leader of great renown,
But his failure to address the issue of climate change, now wears him down.
He laments his mistakes and regrets, as he wanders through this barren ground,
Wishing he had done more to prevent the fate that now surrounds.

As they traverse the circle, Dante and Virgil come across a sight,
A soul being punished for their denial, with all their might.
It is the soul of Aristotle, the philosopher of old,
His failure to address the issue, now leaves him feeling cold.

But in the midst of all this despair and suffering,
A glimmer of hope begins to softly ring.
For some souls, the opportunity for redemption is not gone,
With sincere remorse and action, they can break free from this cycle of wrong.

And so, Dante and Virgil continue on their journey through the Seventh

Circle,
A reminder to us all, that our actions have consequences, and to be mindful, is vital
For the sake of future generations, we must all strive,
To break free from the cycle of denial and truly come alive.

As Dante and Virgil journey deeper into the Seventh Circle,
They come across the soul of Shakespeare, once a master of the written word.
But his failure to address the issue of climate change in his works,
Now leaves him wracked with guilt, his punishment, forever to be blurred.

Next, they encounter the soul of Columbus, a man of great fame,
But his actions led to the destruction of the earth, and now he bears the blame.
He laments his mistakes and regrets, as he wanders through this eternal flame,
Wishing he had been more mindful of the consequences of his aim.

As they continue on their journey, Dante and Virgil come across a soul,
A scientist who failed to speak out against the destruction of the earth as a whole.
It is the soul of Galileo, once a great thinker, now trapped in eternal toll.
His failure to act on the knowledge he had, now takes its toll.

But amidst all this despair, there is still a glimmer of hope,
For those who repent and take action, there is still a way to cope.
For the sake of future generations, we must all strive,
To break free from the cycle of denial, and truly come alive.

And so Dante and Virgil continue on their journey through the Seventh Circle,
A reminder to us all that time is running out, and every action has its ripple.
We must take responsibility for our actions and strive to be mindful,
For the sake of our planet and future generations, this is crucial and vital.

As Dante and Virgil journey through the Seventh Circle,
They come across the soul of Beowulf, once a hero of legendary tale.
But his failure to address the issue of climate change, now leaves him frail,
His reputation and legacy, forever tarnished by his denial.

Next, they encounter the soul of Tesla, a man of great innovation,
But his failure to address the environmental impact of his creations, now leads
to damnation.
He laments his mistakes and regrets, as he wanders through this desolation,
Wishing he had been more mindful of the consequences of his nation.

As they delve deeper into the circle, Dante and Virgil come across a soul,
A leader who failed to take action on climate change, now trapped in this hole.
It is the soul of Putin, once a leader of great power, now trapped in eternal toll,
His failure to act on the issue now takes its toll.

But amidst all this despair and suffering, there is still a glimmer of hope,
For those who repent and take action, there is still a way to cope.
For the sake of future generations, we must all strive,
To break free from the cycle of denial and truly come alive.

And so Dante and Virgil continue on their journey through the Seventh Circle,
A reminder to us all that our actions have consequences, and that being
mindful is crucial.
We must take responsibility for our actions and strive to make a difference,
For the sake of our planet and future generations, this is vital and essential.

14. The Ascent to Purgatory

In the depths of Hell, Dante and Virgil tread,
Guided by the spirit of the great Pushkin, dead.
Through circles of fire and brimstone they pass,
Hearing screams of the damned, a mournful mass.

But as they journey on, a glimmer of hope,
A path to redemption, a way to cope.
As they ascend the mountain of Purgatory, known as 'ka Ding-pynkhuid ba nyngkong'
They see souls that are burdened, but not yet sorry.

The first terrace is that of the proud,
Whose hearts are heavy, their souls bowed.
Their eyes fixed on the ground,
Their penance to walk with heavy bound.

The second terrace is for the envious,
Who green with envy, their souls are heavy.
They gaze upon the light with longing eyes,
But their jealousy will not let them rise.

The third terrace is for the wrathful,
Whose anger consumes, their souls are awful.
They lash out in rage, their spirits wild,
But through penance, they may be reconciled.

The fourth terrace is for the slothful,

Who lay idle, their souls are loathful.
They must climb the steep incline,
To atone for their laziness and be refined.

The fifth terrace is for the avaricious,
Who hoard and hoard, their souls auspicious.
They must give up their wealth and all they own,
To gain forgiveness and a new throne.

As Dante and Virgil continue on their way,
They meet the great Tolstoy and Dostoevsky,
Who guide them through the final terrace,
Where the souls of the gluttonous must face.

The journey is long and the road is steep,
But the souls that seek redemption will find sleep.
For in Purgatory, they can find their way,
To the light of Heaven, where they will stay.

As Dante and Virgil reach the top of the mountain,
They behold the beauty of the eternal fountain.
The souls of the redeemed, now pure and bright,
Shine like stars in the heavens, a sight so right.

They meet the great Gogol and Chekhov,
Who welcome them with open arms, a loving dove.
They are shown the way to the gate of Paradise,
Where the souls of the righteous forever reside.

But before they can enter, they must be cleansed,
Their souls purified, their sins confessed.

They must face the judgment of their deeds,
And accept the punishment that their souls need.

Through the trials and tribulations of their journey,
Dante and Virgil learn humility and mercy.
They understand the importance of redemption,
And the need for forgiveness and atonement.

As they leave the mountain of Purgatory,
They know they have been changed forevermore.
For in the road to redemption, they have found,
The true meaning of life, love and sound.

Thus, the Ascent to Purgatory, the road to redemption,
A journey that all souls must undertake,
To find forgiveness, peace, and eternal salvation,
And to finally be free from the chains of damnation.

As they leave behind the souls of the damned,
They know that they must always be on guard.
For the temptation of sin is ever present,
And the devil's seductions are always persistent.

They remember the lessons learned on the mountain,
And the wisdom shared by the great Dostoevsky, Pushkin, Tolstoy and Gogol's fountain.
They know that they must always strive for perfection,
And to never give in to the temptations of corruption.

The road to redemption is not an easy one,
But with the guidance of Virgil, Pushkin, Tolstoy, Dostoevsky and Gogol, it

can be done.
With each step, they must choose the path of light,
And to never give in to the darkness of night.

As they enter the gates of Paradise,
They understand the true meaning of sacrifice.
For in the end, it is not about wealth or fame,
But about love, forgiveness, and spiritual claim.

And so, the Ascent to Purgatory: The Road to Redemption,
Is a journey that all souls must undertake.
To find forgiveness, peace, and eternal salvation,
And to finally be free from the chains of damnation.

May we all learn from Dante and Virgil's journey,
And find the road to redemption, our souls to flourish.
For in the end, it is not about

15. Purgatory's Terrace of Materialism

In the land of the dead, where souls do dwell,
Dante and Virgil tread, through realms of hell.
But now they climb the mountain of the blessed, known as 'ka Ding-pynkhuid ba ar'
Where Purgatory's Terrace of Materialism, is expressed.

The souls of the materialistic, punished here,
For their earthly sins, in sorrow and fear.
But through penance and prayer, they'll be purified,
And ascend to Heaven, their souls sanctified.

The path is long and steep, the journey hard,
But with Virgil as guide, Dante is not scarred.
They pass by shades of Plutus, the ancient Greek god of wealth,
Whose greed and avarice, brought them to this realm of stealth.

They see the souls of Midas, with golden hands,
Whose love of riches, led to his downfall, in barren lands.
And Croesus, the wealthy king, with his vast treasures,
Whose materialism, brought him nothing but woes and miseries.

As they climb the terrace, Dante and Virgil, converse,
On the nature of greed, and its inverse.
For true happiness, they both agree,
Is found not in material wealth, but in the spiritual and the free.

They reach the top, where the souls are cleansed,
And Dante's journey continues, to Heaven's gate, immense.
For in this terrace, the materialistic souls, have learned,
That true fulfillment, is not to be found, in material earned.

As they leave the terrace, Dante's mind is awash
With the lessons learned, and the wisdom amassed.
For the materialistic souls, have shown him the way
To a life of balance, and a brighter day.

But the journey is not over, as they must proceed,
To the next terrace, where sins of envy are the seed.
And Dante, must face his own demons, deep within,
And learn to let go, of his own envy, and the sins that spin.

But with Virgil by his side, and the souls they've met,
Dante's heart is filled, with a sense of peace and no regret.
For the journey through Purgatory, is one of self-discovery,
And the path to Heaven, is one of true recovery.

So let us all learn, from Dante's tale,
And strive for balance, in our own holy grail.
For the Terrace of Materialism, is just one step,
On the path to enlightenment, and the eternal repose.

As Dante and Virgil continue their journey,
They come upon the terrace of the gluttonous, where souls do bury.
Here, the spirits of those who indulged in excess,
Are punished for their sins of overindulgence and transgress.

They see the shades of Bacchus, the god of wine,

Whose love for pleasure, led to a life of decline.
And Cleopatra, the queen who feasted like a king,
Whose gluttony, led to her downfall, and the end of an era, it would bring.

But as they climb this terrace, Dante sees the light,
That true satisfaction, comes not from excess, but from what's right.
For moderation in all things, is the key,
To a life lived well, and a soul set free.

As they reach the top, the souls are purified,
And Dante's journey continues, towards the ultimate goal, so desired.
For the terrace of gluttony, has taught him the way,
To live in balance, and to find true satisfaction, each and every day.

But still, the journey goes on, as they must proceed,
To the next terrace, where sins of laziness and sloth do breed.
And Dante, must confront his own weaknesses, and strive,
To overcome them, and to truly come alive.

For the journey through Purgatory, is one of self-improvement,
And the path to Heaven, is one of constant movement.
So let us all learn, from Dante's tale,
And strive for progress, and to never fail.

As Dante and Virgil continue on their quest,
They come upon the terrace of the wrathful and the depressed.
Here, the spirits of those consumed by anger and despair,
Are punished for their sins, and made to repair.

They see the shades of Achilles, the warrior great,
Whose wrath led to the downfall of many, and sealed his fate.

And Caesar, the leader, consumed by ambition and pride,
Whose anger and envy, led to his downfall, and a nation divided.

But as they climb this terrace, Dante learns to forgive,
And to let go of anger and resentment, for a life to live.
For true peace and happiness, come from within,
And are not found by lashing out, or giving into sin.

As they reach the top, the souls are purified,
And Dante's journey continues, towards the ultimate goal, so desired.
For the terrace of wrath, has taught him the way,
To live in peace, and to find true happiness, each and every day.

But still, the journey goes on, as they must proceed,
To the next terrace, where sins of lust and envy breed.
And Dante, must confront his own desires, and learn,
To control them, and to let true love, his heart, earn.

For the journey through Purgatory, is one of self-control,
And the path to Heaven, is one of self-discipline and goal.
So let us all learn, from Dante's tale,
And strive for self-control, and to never fail.

As Dante and Virgil approach the final terrace,
They come upon the souls of the slothful, in a state of grace.
Here, the spirits of those who lived a life of ease,
Are punished for their lack of effort, and made to seize.

They see the shades of Odysseus, the hero of old,
Whose laziness, led to delays on his journey, and stories untold.
And Aeneas, who shirked his duty, and delayed his fate,

Whose sloth, led to much suffering, before he could find his mate.

But as they climb this terrace, Dante finds the will to strive,
And to work towards his goals, and to truly come alive.
For true fulfillment, comes from effort and toil,
And to achieve one's dreams, requires discipline and toil.

As they reach the top, the souls are purified,
And Dante's journey comes to an end, as he enters the gates of Heaven, so desired.
For the terrace of sloth, has taught him the way,
To live with purpose, and to find true fulfillment, each and every day.

16. Purgatory's Terrace of Apathy

Upon the Terrace of Apathy, Dante and Virgil tread,
Where souls of those who were indifferent lay in beds, known as 'ka Ding-
pynkhuid ba lai'
The punishment for apathy, a plight most severe,
To purify the souls, and make them whole once more.

They met with souls of Caesar and of Cleopatra's form,
Whose apathy in life had caused a nation to be torn,
And Socrates and Plato, great philosophers of old,
Whose apathy in action left wisdom's tales untold.

They saw the spirits of Martin and of Malala too,
Whose apathy in fighting for what's right, led to a skew,
And Churchill and Mandela, leaders of renown,
Whose apathy in youth, did not lead to freedom's crown.

The souls in this terrace, were made to walk in a line,
Their eyes fixed upon the earth, devoid of spirit and shine,
But as they purged their apathy, they lifted up their gaze,
And towards the heavens, they lifted their hearts in praise.

For in this terrace of Purgatory, they learned the truth,
That apathy in life, leads to an unfulfilled youth,
And only through action, and the pursuit of good,
Can one's soul be truly purged, and in peace understood.

So let us learn from Dante and Virgil's journey here,
To not be apathetic, but to live a life of cheer,
To fight for what is right, and to never lose our fire,
For only then, can we truly ascend, ever higher.

As they journeyed on, they came upon a sight,
The souls of those who were apathetic in the fight,
Against injustice and oppression, they did not speak,
Their silence, a damning sentence, so bleak.

The souls of King Louis and Queen Marie, they found,
Whose apathy in the face of revolution, brought them to the ground,
And Dickens and Shakespeare, whose words could have swayed,
But their apathy, left the poor, in misery portrayed.

They saw the spirits of Mother Teresa and Gandhi,
Whose apathy in their youth, did not lead to victory,
But through action and sacrifice, they made a change,
Their spirits now, no longer in apathy's range.

The souls in this terrace, were made to wear a cloak,
Of feathers, plucked from the wings of a dove, a sad joke,
But as they purged their apathy, the feathers fell away,
And they were given wings, to fly and soar on high today.

For in this terrace of Purgatory, they learned a lesson,
That apathy in the face of injustice, is a mortal transgression,
And only through action, and the pursuit of right,
Can one's soul be truly purified, and in glory take flight.

So let us learn from Dante and Virgil's journey here,

To not be apathetic, but to live a life of cheer,
To fight for what is just, and to never be afraid,
For only then, can we truly ascend, in the heavens arrayed.

As they journeyed deeper, they came across a scene,
Of souls who were apathetic in their personal lives, so lean,
They met with souls of Hemingway and Fitzgerald,
Whose apathy in love, caused their hearts to wizen.

And Byron and Keats, poets of great renown,
Whose apathy in relationships, left them with a heart of stone,
And Picasso and Monet, artists of great skill,
Whose apathy in their personal lives, left their art unfilled.

The souls in this terrace, were made to hold a mirror,
To reflect on their apathetic ways, and their hearts to terror,
But as they purged their apathy, the mirror cracked,
And their hearts were filled with love, and their souls were stacked.

For in this terrace of Purgatory, they learned a truth,
That apathy in one's personal life, brings only uncouth,
And only through love, and the pursuit of self-care,
Can one's soul be truly purged, and in happiness, ensnare.

So let us learn from Dante and Virgil's journey here,
To not be apathetic, in love and life, so dear,
To open our hearts and to nurture our souls,
For only then, can we truly ascend, and reach our goals."

The journey through the terrace of apathy, was long and hard,
But Dante and Virgil's souls, were cleansed and scarred,

For they learned that apathy, in any form, was a sin,
And only through action, love and self-care, could they truly win.

17. The First Sphere of Heaven

As Dante and Virgil embarked on their journey,
They sought to explore the realms of Heaven's glory.
Through the gates of the first sphere they did pass,
Where the souls of those who fought for equality did rest.

The Sphere of Equality was their destination,
known as 'Ka Khet-bneng ba nyngkong'
Where justice and fairness were the foundation.
The souls here were free from all earthly woes,
Their deeds in life had earned them repose.

The first soul they met was named Ashoka,
A ruler from India who had forsaken the sword.
He had spread peace and equality throughout his land,
And now in Heaven, his virtues did expand.

Next, they met a Japanese poet, named Kukai,
Whose words had inspired others to strive for equity.
He had used his pen to champion the cause,
And now in Heaven, his spirit did pause.

As they walked through the sphere,
They saw souls of all nations and cultures,
All united in their quest for justice,
Their deeds in life, now Heaven's treasures.

The souls in this sphere, did not dwell on rank,

For in Heaven, all were equal, with no thanks.
They had lived their lives with love and compassion,
And now in Heaven, they were free from all division.

inspired by the souls they met,
Their hearts filled with hope and regret.
For in their own lives, they too had faltered,
And now they knew, they too could alter.

They saw the souls of Martin and Malcolm,
Whose fight for equality still echoed in them.
They had fought for the rights of the oppressed,
And now in Heaven, their spirits were blessed.

The sphere of Equality was a reminder,
Of the work that still needed to be done.
For though these souls had reached their reward,
Their message still needed to be heard.

As Dante and Virgil left the sphere,
They carried with them the lessons learned.
For in their journey through the realms of Heaven,
They had seen the power of equality and the will of the souls that fought for it
and realized that the fight for justice was never done.

They knew that they too must strive,
To make the world a better place to live.
To work towards equality and justice,
And to let the light of love and compassion give.

For in this sphere, they had seen the truth,

That the souls who fought for equality were not few.
But were present in every culture and nation,
Their deeds in life, a true inspiration.

And so, as Dante and Virgil continued on their way,
They knew that the sphere of Equality would stay.
A guide for them and for all who sought,
To make the world a better never be brought.

To complacency or apathy,
For in the quest for justice, there is no guarantee.
It takes constant effort, and a steadfast will,
To make the world a better place, and to fulfill.

The promise of equality and justice for all,
A task that is never easy, but always worth the call.
For in the end, it is the souls who strive,
Who will find their place in Heaven, and truly thrive.

And so, Dante and Virgil's journey continues,
As they explore the realms of Heaven and its mysteries.
With the guiding them,
As they seek to understand the divine and its realities.

For in the end, it is the quest for truth and righteousness,
That will lead us to our ultimate goal.
To be in harmony with the divine, and find our place,
In the eternal realm, where the souls of the just will roll.

And so, let us all strive towards equality,
And let the light of justice and love shine bright.

For in the end, it is our deeds that will define us,
And bring us to the eternal light of Heaven's light.

18. The Second Sphere of Heaven: The Sphere of Environmentalism

As Dante and Virgil journeyed through the second sphere of Heaven,
They found themselves among the souls of those who fought for the preservation of the Earth.
In this realm, a harmony of nature and spirit was felt,
known as 'Ka Khet-bneng ba ar'
And the souls of environmentalists danced and dwelt.

Rachel Carson, with her book "Silent Spring,"
Fought for the protection of birds and everything.
David Suzuki, with his tireless efforts,
Fought for the rights of nature, and never wavered.

Wangari Maathai, with her Green Belt Movement,
Fought for the rights of women and the environment.
Jane Goodall, with her research on chimpanzees,
Fought for the protection of all animals and their habitats.

Aldo Leopold, with his "Land Ethic,"
Fought for the preservation of land and its ethic.
John Muir, with his love for the Sierra Nevada,
Fought for the protection of all nature, and was a true advocate-a.

Vandana Shiva, with her fight against globalization,
Fought for the rights of farmers and their preservation.

Bill McKibben, with his fight against climate change,
Fought for the preservation of our planet and its range.

Al Gore, with his fight against global warming,
Fought for the preservation of our planet, and its forming.
Kumi Naidoo, with his fight against environmental racism,
Fought for the rights of marginalized communities and their access.

Winona LaDuke, with her fight for indigenous rights,
Fought for the preservation of their land and its lights.
Sylvia Earle, with her ocean conservation efforts,
Fought for the protection of our oceans and their sorts.

And Jadav Payeng, the Molai, with his forest creation,
Fought for the preservation of nature and its preservation.
In this sphere of Heaven, these souls are rewarded,
For their tireless efforts in preserving our planet, and are adored.

And as Dante and Virgil walked among these souls,
They felt a sense of peace, and a sense of role.
For they knew that these environmentalists,
Had fought for the preservation of our planet, and its inhabitants.

They saw Rachel Carson, smiling and serene,
As she looked upon the birds that she had saved from unseen.
David Suzuki, standing tall and proud,
As he looked upon the trees that he had allowed.

Wangari Maathai, surrounded by the green,
As she looked upon the fruits of her labor, so keen.
Jane Goodall, surrounded by chimpanzees,

As she looked upon the research that had changed us.

Aldo Leopold, surrounded by the land,
As he looked upon the ethic that he had planned.
John Muir, surrounded by the mountains,
As he looked upon the nature that he had counted.

Vandana Shiva, surrounded by the farmers,
As she looked upon the rights that she had honored.
Bill McKibben, surrounded by the climate,
As he looked upon the change that he had driven.

Al Gore, surrounded by the earth,
As he looked upon the warming that he had fought.
Kumi Naidoo, surrounded by the marginalized,
As he looked upon the rights that he had advocated.

Winona LaDuke, surrounded by her tribe,
As she looked upon the land that she had preserved.
Sylvia Earle, surrounded by the ocean,
As she looked upon the conservation that she had motioned.

And Jadav Payeng, the Molai, surrounded by the trees,
As he looked upon the forest that he had seized.
In this sphere of Heaven, these souls are at peace,
For their tireless efforts in preserving our planet, will never cease.
As Dante and Virgil leave this realm, they know
That their journey is not over, and their path still glows.
For the preservation of our planet, is a task for all,
And in the end, we will stand tall.
For the preservation of our planet, is a task for all,

And in the end, we will stand tall.
And as we journey through this life,
Let us remember these souls, and their strife.
For they have shown us the way,
To preserve our planet, and make it stay.
For they have shown us the way,
To preserve our planet, and make it stay.
In the end, the preservation of our planet is a task for all,
And in the end, we will stand tall.
In the end, the preservation of our planet is a task for all,
And in the end, we will stand tall.
In the end, the preservation of our planet is a task for all,
And in the end, we will stand tall.
In the end, the preservation of our planet is a task for all,
And in the end, we will stand tall.

19. The Third Sphere of Heaven: The Sphere of Empathy

Through the gates of Pearly white,
Dante and Virgil tread with might,
To the Third Sphere of Heaven's height,
known as 'Ka Khet-bneng ba lai'
Where souls of empathy take flight.

With Virgil as his guiding light,
Dante's journey takes a new plight,
To explore the realm of pure delight,
Where souls of compassion shine bright.

As they walked the path of gold,
Dante's heart began to unfold,
With every step, a new story told,
Of souls who lived for others bold.

The souls in this sphere, Dante saw,
Were those who gave without a flaw,
Who loved and cared for all in awe,
Their compassion, a virtue raw.

Like the Bhagavad Gita's Lord,
These souls embodied empathy's chord,
Their hearts, an ocean deep and broad,
For all, a love that never hoard.

Like the Ramayana's Sita,
Their love for others was a purer criteria,
For them, empathy was the ultimate diva,
Their souls, forever in harmony.

As Dante and Virgil walked on,
They saw the souls in a beautiful song,
Their empathy, a symphony that shone,
Their compassion, a love that never gone.

In the Third Sphere of Heaven's gates,
Dante and Virgil found their fates,
For the journey through empathy awaits,
To reward souls of compassion that elevate.

And as Dante looked above,
He knew the Third Sphere was a realm of love,
Where empathy and compassion reign,
And souls forever, in peace remain.

As Dante and Virgil journeyed on,
They met souls who had long gone,
But their empathy and compassion, still shone,
Their love for others, forever grown.

Like the Mahabharata's Draupadi,
Whose empathy for her husbands, was never shady,
Her love for them, was pure and steady,
A model of compassion, for all to see.

Like the Ramayana's Hanuman,

Whose empathy for Lord Rama, knew no ban,
His devotion, a love that never ran,
A symbol of selflessness, that still stands.

The Third Sphere of Heaven, Dante saw,
Was a realm of purest love and raw,
Where souls of empathy, forever soar,
Their compassion, a virtue that never bore.

As Dante and Virgil reached the end,
They knew the journey was not to pretend,
For the Third Sphere, was a place to befriend,
Where empathy and compassion, never blend.

And so Dante and Virgil bid farewell,
To the Third Sphere, where souls of empathy dwell,
For their journey had come to an end,
But the lessons they learned, will forever blend.

For in the Third Sphere of Heaven, Dante knew,
Lies the path to true empathy and virtue,
Where compassion and love, forever brew,
And souls of empathy, forever renew.

As Dante and Virgil turned to leave,
They couldn't help but feel a sense of grief,
For leaving this realm of purest belief,
Where empathy and compassion never cease.

But as they left, they took with them,
The lessons they had learned, a gem,

Of empathy and compassion, a diadem,
That they would carry with them, in the end.

For in the Third Sphere of Heaven,
Dante and Virgil had been given,
A glimpse of the truest virtue,
That empathy and compassion, were not a fiction.

Like the Indian epic Ramayana,
Which teaches us about empathy and divina,
The Third Sphere of Heaven, was an inspiration,
For us all to strive for empathy and compassion.

And so Dante and Virgil journeyed on,
With empathy and compassion, as their dawn,
For the Third Sphere of Heaven, had shown,
The path to true virtue, had forever grown.

So let us all strive to be like those,
Who in the Third Sphere of Heaven, chose,
To embody empathy and compassion, and compose,
A life of love, that forever glows.

As Dante and Virgil journeyed on,
They knew the Third Sphere had just begun,
To teach them the true meaning of empathy,
And the beauty of compassion, a symphony.

Like the Indian epic Mahabharata,
Which teaches us about empathy and karma,
The Third Sphere of Heaven, was an inspiration,

For us all to strive for empathy and compassion.

For in the Third Sphere of Heaven,
Lies the ultimate reward, the leaven,
For those who embodied empathy,
And lived their lives with compassion.

And so Dante and Virgil walked on,
With empathy and compassion, as their song,
For the Third Sphere of Heaven, had shown,
The path to true virtue, had forever grown.

So let us all strive to be like those,
Who in the Third Sphere of Heaven, chose,
To embody empathy and compassion, and compose,
A life of love, that forever glows.

For in the Third Sphere of Heaven,
Lies the ultimate reward, the leaven,
For those who lived with empathy,
And died with compassion.

And as Dante and Virgil reached the end,
They knew their journey had just begun,
For the Third Sphere of Heaven, would always be,
A reminder of the true virtue of empathy.

20. The Fourth Sphere of Heaven

Through the gates of shining steel,
Dante and Virgil tread with zeal,
To the Fourth Sphere of Heaven's appeal,
known as 'Ka Khet-bneng ba saw'
Where souls of innovation take the wheel.

With Virgil as his guiding light,
Dante's journey takes a new height,
To explore the realm of new insight,
Where souls of progress shine bright.

As they walked the path of chrome,
Dante's mind began to roam,
With every step, a new story told,
Of souls who pushed the boundaries bold.

The souls in this sphere, Dante saw,
Were those who pushed the bar,
Who dared to think beyond the law,
Their innovation, a virtue that stood far.

Like the Archimedes of old,
These souls embodied innovation's mold,
Their minds, an ocean deep and bold,
For all, a spark that never cold.

Like the Galileo of the past,

Their contributions to science, were unsurpassed,
For them, innovation was a virtue that would last,
Their souls, forever in eternity cast.

As Dante and Virgil walked on,
They saw the souls in a beautiful song,
Their innovation, a symphony that shone,
Their contributions, a legacy that never gone.

In the Fourth Sphere of gates,
Dante and Virgil found their fates,
For the journey through innovation awaits,
To reward souls of progress that elevate.

And as Dante looked around,
He saw the souls, in a new found,
Their contributions to technology and science, profound,
Their innovations, a legacy that never bound.

Like the Newton of the past,
Whose contributions to physics, forever will last,
His innovations, a legacy that will surpass,
A model of progress, for all to cast.

Like the Einstein of old,
Whose theories revolutionized the world,
His innovations, a legacy that will behold,
A symbol of progress, that still holds.

The Fourth Sphere of Heaven, Dante saw,
Was a realm of progress and raw,

Where souls of innovation, forever soar
a virtue that never bore.

As Dante and Virgil reached the end,
They knew the journey was not to pretend,
For the Fourth Sphere, was a place to befriend,
Where innovation and progress, never blend.

For in the Fourth Sphere of Heaven, Dante knew,
Lies the path to true innovation and virtue,
Where progress and advancements, forever brew,
And souls of innovation, forever renew.

Like the Leonardo da Vinci,
Whose innovations in art and science, were divine-a,
The Fourth Sphere of Heaven, was an inspiration,
For us all to strive for innovation and progression.

And so Dante and Virgil journeyed on,
With innovation and progress, as their dawn,
For the Fourth Sphere of Heaven, had shown,
The path to true virtue, had forever grown.

For in the Fourth Sphere of Heaven,
Lies the ultimate reward, the leaven,
For those who pushed the boundaries of knowledge,
And contributed to scientific and technological advancements.

Like the Marie Curie of the past,
Whose innovations in science, forever will last,
Her contributions, a legacy that will surpass,

A model of progress, for all to cast.

Like the Steve Jobs of old,
Whose innovations in technology, forever bold,
His contributions, a legacy that will behold,
A symbol of progress, that still holds.

And as Dante and Virgil looked back,
They knew that the journey was not a hack,
For the Fourth Sphere of Heaven, had opened a crack,
For them to see the true value of innovation and progress.

Like the Alexander Graham Bell,
Whose innovations in communication, forever dwell,
His contributions, a legacy that will tell,
A model of progress, for all to excel.

Like the Thomas Edison of old,
Whose innovations in electricity, forever bold,
His contributions, a legacy that will behold,
A symbol of progress, that still holds.

Like the Nikola Tesla of the past,
Whose innovations in electricity, forever will last,
His contributions, a legacy that will surpass,
A model of progress, for all to cast.

Like the Wright Brothers of old,
Whose innovations in aviation, forever bold,
Their contributions, a legacy that will behold,
A symbol of progress, that still holds.

Like the Ada Lovelace of old,
Whose innovations in computer science, forever bold,
Her contributions, a legacy that will behold,
A symbol of progress, that still holds.

Like the Tim Berners-Lee of the past,
Whose innovations in the World Wide Web, forever will last,
His contributions, a legacy that will surpass,
A model of progress, for all to cast.

Like the Alan Turing of the past,
Whose innovations in computing, forever will last,
His contributions, a legacy that will surpass,
A model of progress, for all to cast.

The Fourth Sphere of Heaven, Dante saw,
Was a realm of progress and raw,
Where souls of innovation, forever soar,
Their contributions, a virtue that never bore.

As Dante and Virgil reached the end,
They knew the journey was not to pretend,
For the Fourth Sphere, was a place to befriend,
Where innovation and progress, never blend.

And so Dante and Virgil bid farewell,
To the Fourth Sphere, where souls of innovation dwell,
For their journey had come to an end,
But the lessons they learned, will forever blend.

For in the Fourth Sphere of Heaven, Dante knew,
Lies the path to true innovation and virtue,
Where progress and advancements, forever brew,
And souls of innovation, forever renew.

So let us all strive to be like those,
Who in the Fourth Sphere of Heaven, chose,
To embody innovation and progress, and compose,
A life of advancements, that forever glows.

21. The Fifth Sphere of Heaven: The Sphere of Community

Through the gates of gold and gleam,
Dante and Virgil walked with a dream,
To the Fifth Sphere of Heaven's realm,
known as 'Ka Khet-bneng ba san'
Where souls of community, forever helm.

With Virgil as his guiding star,
Dante's journey took him afar,
To explore the realm of community,
Where souls of togetherness, forever free.

As they walked the path of light,
Dante's eyes beheld a sight,
Of souls who worked day and night,
To build and strengthen communities, with all their might.

The souls in this sphere, Dante saw,
Were those who gave without a flaw,
Who worked for the common good,
Their community, their ultimate hood.

Like the Greek philosopher Aristotle,
These souls embodied community's ritual,
Their hearts, a well of wisdom, with a missile,
For all, a love that never dwindle.

Like the Egyptian queen Cleopatra,
Their love for their community, was a purer criteria,
For them, community was the ultimate diva,
Their souls, forever in harmony.

As Dante and Virgil walked on,
They saw the souls in a beautiful song,
Their community work, a symphony that shone,
Their togetherness, a love that never gone.

In the Fifth Sphere of Heaven's gates,
Dante and Virgil found their fates,
For the journey through community awaits,
To reward souls of togetherness, that elevate.

And as Dante looked above,
He knew the Fifth Sphere was a realm of love,
Where community and togetherness reign,
And souls forever, in peace remain.

As Dante and Virgil journeyed on,
They met souls who had long gone,
But their community work, still shone,
Their love for others, forever grown.

A symbol of community, that still glimmers.

The Fifth Sphere of Heaven, Dante saw,
Was a realm of purest love and raw,
Where souls of community, forever soar,
Their togetherness, a virtue that never bore.

As Dante and Virgil turned to leave,
They couldn't help but feel a sense of relief,
For leaving this realm of purest belief,
Where community and togetherness never cease.

But as they left, they took with them,
The lessons they had learned, a gem,
Of community and togetherness, a diadem,
That they would carry with them, in the end.

For in the Fifth Sphere of Heaven,
Dante and Virgil had been given,
A glimpse of the truest virtue,
That community and togetherness, were not a fiction.

Like the Indian epic Mahabharata,
Which teaches us about community and karma,
The Fifth Sphere of Heaven, was an inspiration,
For us all to strive for community and togetherness.

Like the Chinese philosopher Confucius,
These souls embodied community's focus,
Their hearts, a well of wisdom, with a bonus,
For all, a love that never loses.

Like the Indian leader Mahatma Gandhi,
Their love for their community, was a purer criteria,
For them, community was the ultimate diva,
Their souls, forever in harmony.

As Dante and Virgil walked on,
They saw the souls in a beautiful song,
Their community work, a symphony that shone,
Their togetherness, a love that never gone.

Like the American leader Martin Luther King,
Whose empathy for his community, knew no sting,
His devotion, a love that never cling,
A model of selflessness, that still rings.

Like the leader Nelson Mandela,
Whose empathy for his nation, knew no scandal,
His devotion, a love that never scandal,
A symbol of community, that still stands tall.

Like the Egyptian leader Anwar Sadat,
Whose empathy for his nation, knew no spat,
His devotion, a love that never spat,
A model of selflessness, that still sat.

Like the Indian leader Jawaharlal Nehru,
Whose empathy for his community, knew no blue,
His devotion, a love that never blue,
A symbol of community, that still grew.

And so Dante and Virgil journeyed on,
With community and togetherness, as their dawn,
For the Fifth Sphere of Heaven, had shown,
The path to true virtue, had forever grown.

So let us all strive to be like those,

Who in the Fifth Sphere of Heaven, chose,

To embody community and togetherness, and compose,

A life of love, that forever glows.

For in the Fifth Sphere of Heaven,

Lies the ultimate reward, the leaven,

For those who embodied community,

And lived their lives with togetherness.

And as Dante and Virgil reached the end,

They knew their journey had just begun,

For the Fifth Sphere of Heaven, would always be,

A reminder of the true virtue of community.

For in the Fifth Sphere of Heaven, Dante knew,

Lies the path to true community and virtue,

Where togetherness and love, forever brew,

And souls of community, forever renew.

And as they left the Fifth Sphere,

Dante and Virgil felt a sense of cheer,

For they knew that the journey through community,

Was a reminder of the importance of empathy and togetherness.

And so they continued on their journey,

With the lessons of the Fifth Sphere, in a hurry,

To spread the message of community and togetherness,

For a better world, for all, with empathy as the key.

22. The Sixth Sphere of Heaven: The Sphere of Education

Dante, with guide Virgil in tow,
Set forth upon the journey bright and slow
To the Sixth Sphere of Heaven's ethereal shore,
known as 'Ka Khet-bneng ba hynriew'
Where knowledge reigns, and wisdom is adored.

Through the vast expanse of the starry skies,
They flew on the wings of truth and wise
Guided by the light of the eternal flame
Towards the realm of education and fame.

As they reached the gates of the sphere divine,
They were greeted by Socrates and Plato's shine,
The great philosophers of ancient Greece
Who led them through the halls of knowledge and peace.

They walked through the halls of learning and art
Where the souls of scholars and teachers depart,
And met the likes of Confucius and Aristotle
Who shared their wisdom and knowledge with a sequel.

They came upon the halls of literature
Where Homer, Shakespeare and Milton's features
Were etched in marble, and their words were sung
By the choir of souls, in eternal tongues.

They saw the halls of science and math
Where Galileo, Newton and Hawking's path
Were honored, and the mysteries of the universe
Were unlocked for the souls to traverse.

As Dante and Virgil journeyed through the sphere
They were awestruck by the knowledge that was here,
And realized that the pursuit of education
Is the key to the soul's liberation.

As they journeyed further through the sphere,
They met the souls of educators dear,
The likes of Maria Montessori and John Dewey
Who taught the young to think and play.

They came upon the halls of language and speech,
Where the souls of Chaucer, Milton, and Yeats teach,
The beauty of words and the power of expression
To the souls in search of self-expression.

They walked through the halls of history,
Where the souls of Herodotus and Thucydides,
narrated the tales of the past,
And the lessons that forever will last.

They came upon the halls of technology,
Where the souls of Ada Lovelace and Steve Jobs,
Lead the way, in the advancement of mankind,
Towards a future that is bright and kind.

They walked through the halls of art and culture,

Where the souls of Picasso and Beethoven nurture,
The creative spirit and the love for beauty
To the souls in search of their own duty.

They came upon the halls of philosophy,
Where the souls of Kant and Descartes,
Debated the nature of reality
And the quest for understanding, truly be.

They saw the halls of social science,
Where the souls of Durkheim and Weber,
Explored the complexities of human society
And the role of education in shaping diversity.

As Dante and Virgil left the sphere,
They felt the weight of all they had heard and seen here,
For they knew that education is the key,
To unlocking the mysteries of humanity.

As they soared through the ethereal skies,
They couldn't help but reflect on the lessons and sighs,
Of the souls they had met in the sphere of education,
And the impact they had on the world's civilization.

They thought of the teachers who had touched their lives,
The mentors who had guided them through their struggles and strives,
The educators who had ignited their passion for learning,
And the knowledge they had been yearning.

They realized that the sphere of education,
Is not just a place of reward and adulation,

But a place where the souls continue to learn,
And the pursuit of knowledge, forever burn.

As they reached the end of their journey,
They knew that their quest for knowledge was not temporary,
For the pursuit of wisdom is a lifelong endeavor,
And the rewards, forever and ever.

But as they prepared to leave, a voice divine,
Echoed through the halls, a call, a sign,
"Dante, dear poet, your journey is not done,
For there are more spheres to explore, more knowledge to be won."

And so, Dante and Virgil set forth once more,
To continue their journey, to explore and adore,
The realms of the heavens and the secrets they hold,
For the quest for knowledge is a story untold.

They knew that their journey was far from over,
That there were more lessons to be discovered,
More wisdom to be gained, more knowledge to be earned,
For the pursuit of education, forever burns.

As they journeyed on, they came across
The sphere of the arts, where beauty was the boss,
Where the souls of da Vinci, Monet, and Mozart
Created masterpieces that still touch the heart.

They walked through the halls of mathematics,
Where the souls of Euclid, Gauss, and Pythagoras,
Unveiled the secrets of numbers and space,

And the beauty of the universe's face.

They came upon the halls of medicine,
Where the souls of Hippocrates, Pasteur, and Galen,
Healed the sick and saved lives with their art,
And the pursuit of knowledge, played a big part.

As Dante and Virgil journeyed through the spheres,
They came to realize the importance of their peers,
For in the pursuit of knowledge, one must never rest,
For the quest for wisdom, is truly the best.

As they traveled through the spheres of light,
They were overcome by a sense of might,
For the souls they encountered were truly great,
And their contributions to the world, truly weight.

They walked through the halls of psychology,
Where the souls of Jung, Freud, and Skinner,
Explored the depths of the human mind,
And the secrets of the soul, they did find.

They came upon the halls of ecology,
Where the souls of Rachel Carson, and Jane Goodall,
Fought to protect the natural world,
And the balance of life and earth, unfurled.

They walked through the halls of agriculture,
Where the souls of Borlaug, and Verghese Kurien,
Fed the world and revolutionized farming,
And the quest for knowledge, kept them charming.

They came upon the halls of law,
Where the souls of Gandhi, Martin Luther King,
Fought for justice and equality,
And their legacies, forever will ring.

As Dante and Virgil journeyed through the spheres,
They came to understand the importance of their peers,
For in the pursuit of knowledge, one must strive for good,
For the quest for wisdom, is the path to a better hood.

As they reached the highest spheres,
They were greeted by the souls of pioneers,
The likes of Marie Curie, and Stephen Hawking,
Who pushed the boundaries of human thinking.

They walked through the halls of space exploration,
Where the souls of Neil Armstrong, and Yuri Gagarin,
Unveiled the mysteries of the cosmos,
And the potential of mankind, truly awesome.

They came upon the halls of innovation,
Where the souls of Jobs, and Gates, and Zuckerberg,
Changed the way we live and communicate,
And the quest for knowledge, truly elevate.

As Dante and Virgil journeyed through the spheres,
They came to realize the significance of their peers,
For in the pursuit of knowledge, one must never stop,
For the quest for wisdom, is the key to unlocking the top.

As they reached the final sphere,
They were met with a sight so dear,
The souls of the greatest educators of all time,
Standing before them in a line.

They saw the likes of Plato and Aristotle,
Confucius and Socrates,
Who had dedicated their lives to teaching,
And had left a legacy that was reaching.

They walked through the halls of enlightenment,
Where the souls of Da Vinci and Galileo,
Unveiled the mysteries of the world,
And the power of education unfurled.

They came upon the halls of progress,
Where the souls of Darwin and Einstein,
Changed the way we think and live,
And the quest for knowledge, truly give.

As Dante and Virgil reached the end of their journey,
They knew that the pursuit of knowledge was a lifelong story,
For the quest for wisdom is an eternal endeavor,
And the rewards of education, truly forever.

And so they bid farewell to the sphere of education,
With a heart full of gratitude and inspiration,
For the journey of knowledge never ends,
And the quest for wisdom, forever transcends."

23. The Seventh Sphere of Heaven: The Sphere of Creativity

As Dante and Virgil journey through the seventh sphere,
known as 'Ka Khet-bneng ba hynniew'
They are greeted by the souls of those who've held dear,
The arts and culture, and contributed so much,
To the beauty and expression of the human touch.

They see Michelangelo, the master of marble and clay,
Whose sculptures and paintings still take our breath away,
Pablo Picasso, the cubist who changed the way we see,
Vincent van Gogh, whose post-impressionist paintings set free,
The colors of the soul and emotions within,
Salvador Dalí, the surrealist who delved deep within,
The human psyche to reveal the strange and surreal,
Frida Kahlo, the Mexican painter whose life was a duel,
Of pain and passion, reflected in her art,
Claude Monet, the impressionist who captured the heart,
Of nature and light in his masterful strokes,
Mark Rothko and Jackson Pollock, the abstract expressionists who awoke,
The senses and emotions with their bold and expressive art,
Marcel Duchamp, the Dadaist who played with the smart,
Concepts of art and reality, and challenged the norm,
Bob Dylan, the folk singer whose songs were a storm,
Of protest and emotion, and spoke to the soul,
John Lennon and Freddie Mercury, musicians whose rock and roll,
Still echoes through the ages, and reaches the heart,
Miles Davis, the jazz master whose trumpet did start,

A revolution in music, and pushed the boundaries of sound,

Ludwig van Beethoven, the classical composer who never let bound,

His passion for music, and created masterpieces that stand the test of time,

Wolfgang Amadeus Mozart, the prodigy who's symphonies and rhymes,

Are still celebrated and loved,

Johann Sebastian Bach, the master of harmony, whose music above,

All others is still celebrated and loved,

Tchaikovsky, the romantic composer whose music is still celebrated and loved.

George Gershwin, the jazz and classical composer,

Stephen Sondheim, the Broadway master who was a closer,

To the hearts of his audience, with every song he wrote,

Virginia Woolf, the modernist novelist who wrote,

With a feminist perspective, and her prose afloat,

James Joyce, the modernist who pushed the bounds,

Samuel Beckett, the playwright who astounded,

With his avant-garde style and his wit so dry,

Langston Hughes, the Harlem Renaissance poet who never denied,

The African American experience and its beauty,

Maya Angelou, the memoirist and activist who portrayed,

The struggles and triumphs of her people with grace,

Oscar Wilde, the playwright and novelist with a face,

Full of wit and irony, and a style all his own,

Edgar Allan Poe, the gothic master who shone,

With his tales of the macabre and his poetry so dark,

F. Scott Fitzgerald, the jazz age novelist who left a mark,

On literature with his insight into the human soul,

Ernest Hemingway, the modernist who made his role,

In literature one of simplicity and truth,

Toni Morrison, the Pulitzer Prize-winner who uncouth,

The complexities of the human experience with her pen,

All these souls in the seventh sphere, where art begins again.

And as Dante and Virgil continue on their journey,
They are awed by the beauty and art that surrounds them in a flurry,
For in the seventh sphere, the souls of these great artists,
Are forever rewarded for their contributions and persist,
In creating beauty and meaning in the world,
Their works standing the test of time, forever unfurled,
As a testament to the human spirit and its ability to create,
And inspire others to do the same, to elevate,
The world through the power of art and creativity,
In the seventh sphere of heaven, where true beauty will always be.

As Dante and Virgil continue on their journey, they come across
A group of souls who are singing and dancing, lost
In the joy of creativity, and they realize that this sphere
Is a place where art and culture are held dear.

They see Michelangelo, the master of marble and clay,
Whose sculptures and paintings still take our breath away,
Pablo Picasso, the cubist who changed the way we see,
Vincent van Gogh, whose post-impressionist paintings set free,
The colors of the soul and emotions within,
Salvador Dalí, the surrealist who delved deep within,
The human psyche to reveal the strange and surreal,
Frida Kahlo, the Mexican painter whose life was a duel,
Of pain and passion, reflected in her art,
Claude Monet, the impressionist who captured the heart,
Of nature and light in his masterful strokes,
Mark Rothko and Jackson Pollock, the abstract expressionists who awoke,
The senses and emotions with their bold and expressive art,

Marcel Duchamp, the Dadaist who played with the smart,

Concepts of art and reality, and challenged the norm,

Bob Dylan, the folk singer whose songs were a storm,

Of protest and emotion, and spoke to the soul,

John Lennon and Freddie Mercury, musicians whose rock and roll,

Still echoes through the ages, and reaches the heart,

Miles Davis, the jazz master whose trumpet did start,

A revolution in music, and pushed the boundaries of sound,

Ludwig van Beethoven, the classical composer who never let bound,

His passion for music, and created masterpieces that stand the test of time,

Wolfgang Amadeus Mozart, the prodigy who's symphonies and rhymes,

Are still celebrated and loved,

Johann Sebastian Bach, the master of harmony, whose music above,

All others is still celebrated and loved,

Tchaikovsky, the romantic composer whose music is still celebrated and loved.

As they witness the beauty and creativity of these souls,

Dante and Virgil realize that this is where true beauty unfolds,

And they are humbled and inspired by the power of art,

To elevate the human spirit and touch the heart.

And so they continue on their journey,

Knowing that the seventh sphere is where true beauty will always be,

A place where art and culture are celebrated and revered,

And where the human spirit can be truly cleared.

24. The Final Sphere: The Empyrean of Unity

As Dante and Virgil continue on their journey,
They are struck by the beauty and serenity,
Of the Empyrean, where the souls of the blessed,
known as 'Ka Khet-bneng ba khatduh'
Are united in the ultimate understanding of love and rest.

They see the Dove, a symbol of peace and unity,
Its wings spread wide, as if to set free,
All the souls in the Empyrean, from the bonds of pain and strife,
And remind them that true unity is the ultimate prize.

The Lotus, a symbol of enlightenment and spiritual growth,
Representing the journey towards inner peace and unity,
Its petals open, as if to show,
That true unity is a state of being we all should know.

The Om, a sacred symbol of Hinduism,
Representing the ultimate reality and unity of all things,
Its sound echoing through the Empyrean,
Reminding the souls of their spiritual being.

The Infinity symbol, representing the infinite and eternal nature of love and
unity,
A reminder that true unity lasts forever, it will never be fleeting.

The Star of David, the symbol of Judaism,

Representing the connection and unity between God and humanity,
A reminder that true unity is not just among human beings but also with God.

The Ankh, an ancient symbol of Egypt,
Representing life and eternal love,
A reminder that true unity is not just a temporary state, but a permanent one.

The Yin-Yang, symbolizing the balance and unity of opposite forces,
A reminder that true unity is found in the balance of all things.

The Circle, representing wholeness, completeness and unity,
A reminder that true unity is found in embracing all aspects of ourselves.

The Celtic Knot, symbolizing interconnectedness and unity of all things,
A reminder that true unity is found in the interconnectedness of all things.

The Peace Sign, the iconic symbol of peace and unity,
Representing the hope for a world without conflict,
A reminder that true unity is found in the absence of war and strife.

The Heart, the universal symbol of love and unity,
A reminder that true unity is found in the love that we share with one another.

The Hands of Unity, symbolizing coming together and working towards a
common goal,
A reminder that true unity is found in the actions we take to come together.

The Tree of Life, representing the interconnectedness and unity of all living
things,
A reminder that true unity is found in the interconnectedness of all life.

The Rainbow, symbolizing hope, unity and acceptance of diversity,
A reminder that true unity is found in the acceptance and celebration of diversity.

The Unity Candle, used in marriage, representing the coming together in love,
A reminder that true unity is found in the love and commitment we share with others.

As Dante and Virgil continue their journey,
They come across a group of souls, who are in a state of serenity,
They are surrounded by symbols of unity and love,
The Dove, the Lotus, the Om, the Infinity symbol, the Star of David above.

They see the Ankh, the Yin-Yang, the Circle,
The Celtic Knot, the Peace Sign, the Heart, the Hands of Unity,
The Tree of Life, the Rainbow, the Unity Candle,
All symbols of unity and peace, that are truly grand.

These souls are blessed, for they have come to understand,
That true unity is not just a command,
But a state of being, that we all can achieve,
Through love, peace, and understanding, we all can believe.

As Dante and Virgil look upon these souls,
They see the love and unity that makes them whole,
And they understand that true unity is not just a concept,
But a state of being, that we all can accept.

And as they continue on their journey,
Dante and Virgil are filled with hope and serenity,
For they know that true unity is within reach,

And that the Empyrean is where all souls will eventually find peace.

As Dante and Virgil reach the end of their journey,
They realize that the Empyrean is not just a place of heavenly glory,
But a state of being, a state of unity,
A state where all souls are free from animosity.

They understand that true unity is not just a concept,
But a state of being that we can all reach,
Through love, peace, and understanding,
We can all find unity and live in a state of commanding.

The symbols that they have encountered,
The Dove, the Lotus, the Om, the Infinity symbol, the Star of David,
The Ankh, the Yin-Yang, the Circle,
The Celtic Knot, the Peace Sign, the Heart, the Hands of Unity,
The Tree of Life, the Rainbow, the Unity Candle,
All remind us that true unity is not just a fable.

It is a state of being that we can all achieve,
If we open our hearts and minds, we can all believe,
In the power of unity and love,
And in the Empyrean, find peace from above.

And as Dante and Virgil bid farewell,
To the Empyrean, they know that their journey has been well,
For they have come to understand,
That true unity is the ultimate goal, and it's not just a command.

25. The End of the Journey: The Return to Earth

As Dante and Virgil reach the end of their journey,
known as 'Ka Jingkhot khiew ja ing'
They look back on the trials and tribulations they've seen,
From the 21ˢᵗ-century Hell of war and greed,
To the purgatory of mistakes and misdeeds.

They remember the souls they've met,
The politicians and leaders who have sold their debt,
To power and wealth, leaving the masses in despair,
In the abyss of 21ˢᵗ century hell, where souls are ensnared.

They recall the purgatory of the meek,
Where the souls of the lost and the weak,
Are punished for their ignorance and apathy,
In a cycle of rebirth, where they strive for empathy.

And they remember the heaven of the blessed,
Where the souls of the creative and the best,
Are forever rewarded for their contributions and persist,
In creating beauty and meaning in the world, their works standing the test of time, forever unfurled.

As they return to Earth, Dante and Virgil,
Take with them the lessons learned, the memories that will unfurl,
For they understand that the journey of life,
Is a constant struggle, a constant strife.

But with the lessons learned and the wisdom gained,
They know that they can strive for a better world, without any strain,
For they have seen the depths of Hell, the trials of Purgatory,
And the beauty of Heaven, and they know that the journey is necessary.

As they walk back to the world of men,
They know that the journey never truly ends,
For the struggles and trials of life,
Will always be there, causing strife.

But with the lessons learned from the journey through the spheres,
They know that they can strive for a better world, with no fear,
For they understand that unity and love,
Are the keys to a world free of the darkness above.

And as they walk back to the world of men,
They realize that it is not the end,
For the journey of life is a constant cycle,
And they will continue to strive for a world of peace, without any hassle.

Dante and Virgil, with the knowledge they've gained,
Will continue to spread the message, to enlighten and sustain,
For they understand that the journey of life is not a one-time trip,
It's an ongoing quest, where one's soul is forever equipped.

And as they continue on their journey,
Dante and Virgil's legacy will forever be remembered,
For they have shown us that the journey through the spheres,
Is a journey towards unity, love and peace, which will forever be ours.

As they return to Earth, Dante and Virgil,
Take with them the memories of the souls they've met,
Names etched in their minds, forever to be remembered,
Like Socrates and Plato, who in wisdom were surrendered.

The poets and artists, like Shakespeare and Dante,
Who's works continue to inspire, to enlighten and enchant,
The scientists and inventors, like Einstein and Edison,
Whose contributions have shaped the world, and continue to feed on.

The leaders and activists, like Martin Luther King and Gandhi,
Who fought for justice and equality, with their words and actions so handy.

The journey through the spheres has taught them well,
That the path to true unity and peace is long and dwell,
But with the lessons learned and the wisdom gained,
They know that they can strive for a better world, without any strain.

As they return to Earth, Dante and Virgil,
Will continue to spread the message of unity and love, that will unfurl,
For the journey towards a better world, never truly ends,
But with the knowledge gained, it can be achieved, by all and for all, amen.

26. The Legacy of The Divine Comedy of the 21st Century

As Dante and Virgil embark on a new journey,

Through the legacy of The Divine Comedy in the 21ˢᵗ century,

They see the impact and influence it has had,

On society and culture, an impact that's not just a fad.

They come across the works of "Dante's Descendant" a new author,

Whose writing draws inspiration from The Divine Comedy,

And explores the themes of love, redemption, and unity,

In a modern context, giving a new perspective to the story.

They also see the influence of The Divine Comedy,

On the works of "The Inferno Poet" a renowned poet of this century,

Whose poetry delves into the depths of human suffering,

And the search for redemption, much like Dante's.

As they journey through the halls of academia,

They encounter "The Divine Comedy Scholar" a renowned professor,

Whose research and analysis of the poem,

Has helped to deepen the understanding of its themes and poem.

In the art world, they see "The Divine Visionary" a painter,

Whose works are inspired by the imagery and symbolism of The Divine Comedy,

And how it continues to inspire and influence contemporary art,

Reminding us of the enduring legacy of this classic work of art.

In the realm of music, they come across "The Divine Composer" a musician,
Whose compositions draw inspiration from the poem,
And explore its themes of love, redemption, and unity,
In a modern context, reminding us of the poem's versatility.

As Dante and Vir gil continue their journey,
They see the impact of The Divine Comedy in literature and philosophy,
They encounter "The Divine Thinker" a renowned philosopher,
Whose ideas and concepts are deeply influenced by the poem.

They also see the influence of The Divine Comedy,
On the works of "The Divine Novelist" a renowned novelist of this century,
Whose novels explore the human condition,
And the search for meaning and purpose, much like Dante's.

As they journey through the world of film,
They encounter "The Divine Filmmaker" a renowned director,
Whose films are inspired by the imagery and symbolism of The Divine
Comedy,
And how it continues to inspire and influence contemporary cinema,
Reminding us of the enduring legacy of this classic work.

In the theatre, they see "The Divine Playwright" a playwright,
Whose plays are inspired by the themes and characters of The Divine Comedy,
And how it continues to inspire and influence contemporary theatre,
Reminding us of the enduring legacy of this classic work.

As Dante and Virgil reach the end of their journey,
They understand that The Divine Comedy's legacy is not just a story,
But an enduring influence on society and culture,
Reminding us of the power of love, redemption, and unity for ever.

As Dante and Virgil reflect on their journey,
They realize that The Divine Comedy's legacy is not just a fleeting thing,
But an enduring influence that has stood the test of time,
And continues to inspire and shape society and culture, in its prime.

They see how it has influenced art, literature, music, and philosophy,
And how its themes of love, redemption, and unity,
Are still relevant and relatable to people today,
Proving the poem's timelessness, in every way.

They also see how it has inspired new interpretations and adaptations,
Giving new perspectives and insights to the poem's themes and messages,
And how it continues to spark new discussions and debates,
Proving its enduring relevance in contemporary society's states.

As they bid farewell to their journey,
Dante and Virgil are filled with a sense of awe and pride,
For they have come to understand,
That The Divine Comedy's legacy is not just a fleeting thing,
But an enduring influence that will always be a lasting thing.

27. The Divine Comedy of the 21st Century and Modern Interpretations

As Dante and Virgil embark on this new journey,

They find themselves in a world that's vastly different and blurry,

For this is the 21st century, and the Divine Comedy,

Has taken on new forms, and its relevance is no longer a mystery.

They see modern interpretations of the classic tale,

With contemporary themes, that are sure to unveil,

The challenges facing the world today,

And the relevance of the Divine Comedy in a modern way.

They meet "Beatire", a playwright who adapts the story,

To reflect the struggles of the marginalized and the poor,

"Vortex", a filmmaker, whose film version is a commentary,

On the state of politics and power, and its impact on society's core.

"Siren" a poet, whose verses bring to life,

The journey of the soul, and the inner strife,

"Echo", a musician, whose songs reflect,

The human condition, and the search for true respect.

As Dante and Virgil witness these modern adaptations,

They realize that the Divine Comedy is not just a story from ages,

But a timeless tale, that's still relevant today,

As it addresses the human condition, in every which way.

They see how these modern interpretations,
Speak to the challenges facing the world today,
And how they offer hope and understanding,
To those who seek it, in their own way.

And as Dante and Virgil reach the end of this journey,
They realize that the Divine Comedy is not just a work of literature, but a mirror,
Reflecting the human condition, in all its forms,
And providing guidance and understanding, in these trying times and storms.

They understand that the Divine Comedy,
Is not just a story from the past, but a tale that's forever alive,
And that its relevance will always be,
As long as there are human hearts that strive.

For the Divine Comedy is not just a work of art,
But a reflection of the human heart,
And its message of love, redemption and unity,
Will always resonate, and be a guide in the dark.

And as Dante and Virgil bid farewell,
To this new journey, they know that they've been well,
For they have come to understand,
That the Divine Comedy is not just a classic, but a timeless brand.

As Dante and Virgil reflect on their journey,
They see how the Divine Comedy, in its modern interpretation,
Is a reminder that we are all on a journey,
A journey towards understanding, love and unity.

It's a reminder that the challenges facing the world today,
Are not new, they've been there since time began,
And the Divine Comedy offers a path,
To navigate through these challenges, and to understand.

It reminds us that the search for love and redemption,
Is a universal human experience, that needs no exemption,
And that the message of unity and peace,
Is a timeless one, that will never cease.

And as Dante and Virgil set out on their journey once more,
They take with them, the lessons they've learned before,
For the Divine Comedy, in its modern interpretation,
Is a reminder that the human journey towards unity and love, is an ongoing sensation.

As Dante and Virgil continue on their journey,
They remember the words of the modern interpreters,
And how their works reminded them of the importance,
Of the Divine Comedy in today's world and its significance.

They see the relevance of the story,
In addressing the issues of the present and the glory,
Of the human spirit in its quest for understanding,
And the power of love in bringing unity and bonding.

They understand that the Divine Comedy,
Is not just a classic work of literature, but a story,
That speaks to the human condition in every age,
And offers guidance and hope, on life's journey, in every page.

As they journey on, they also realize,

That the Divine Comedy is not just about the afterlife,

But about the human experience, in this life,

And the power of love, redemption and unity, to overcome strife.

And so, as they come to the end of their journey,

Dante and Virgil are filled with a sense of joy and serenity,

For they have come to understand,

That the Divine Comedy is a timeless masterpiece, and a journey of discovery

and a command.

Thank You

Khublei shi hajar nguh

I Am

As I, a breviloquent raptor, wield A lever, with naught else to my design, I generate tones for the aural field In this prosaic orb we call mankind. My actions, though, are but a small part Of forces far beyond my control, For nature holds the key to each chart And sets the laws that govern the whole. But still, I am compelled to explore The workings of this vast machinery, To seek the truth that lies at core And find the answers to humanity. Though some may call it quest I'll seek the truth, with no time to rest.

About The Author

"Mawphniang, Napoleon of Syadheh, From Ri Bhoi District in Meghalaya, A soul ever-striving, ne'er at ease, With boundless curiosity and verve. He embraces new ideas with open mind, And ventures boldly into unknown lands, Passionately seeking all that life may find, And making use of time's fleeting sands. His inquisitive nature knows no bounds, As he seeks answers to life's enigmas, Though not pretending to have all profound, He simply lives, without life's drama. He cherishes the small things in this sphere, And on a journey of self-discovery, He writes his story, never to fear, Making most of life, ever-unfurled."

P.C : Clarissa Candace Giri

www.ingramcontent.com/pod-product-compliance
Lightning Source LLC
Chambersburg PA
CBHW021548150726
47990CB00006B/2441